Slaying Dragons

Quotes, Poetry, & a few Short Stories
for Every Day of the Year

*Congratulations on
winning a copy of my
book. I truly hope you
enjoy it.*

— Richelle E. Goodrich

Slaying Dragons

Quotes, Poetry, & a few Short Stories for Every Day of the Year

Written by
Richelle E. Goodrich

Dedicated to my son, Alexander
Be fearless in the pursuit of your dreams.

TABLE OF CONTENTS

When it comes to fighting for your dreams, be a dragon. Breathe fire.

-Richelle E. Goodrich

JANUARY

— Bakunawa —
The dragon that swallows the moon whole.

January 1st

There are trials in life that feel as tremendous as
a quest to slay dragons. These trials are
daunting. They require hard work,
determination, and courage. But when the
dragon is finally slain, the relief is immense.

January 2nd

It is tempting to quit striving toward a goal when
you have neither the time, the resources, the
support, the means, nor perhaps the confidence in
talent to reach the level of standing you wish to
reach. But these are not reasons to quit. Move
forward anyway. Try your best. Put what little
you do have into accomplishing what you can,
because along the way you may attain a portion
of what you feel is lacking. And owning a
portion of a dream is better than owning no
dream at all. Never give up.

January 3rd

Bad habits are demons that often push us into
isolation because they know that in our
loneliness they stand little chance of being
overcome.

January 4th

Habits grow like dragons if you feed them.

January 5th

Bad habits are spiraling slides that drag you
round and round down the narrowing end of a
cone that eventually ends up in a dark, tight,
confining spot.

Good habits are hooked wings that steadily grow
in girth and strength. At first, they grasp and
climb until those beautiful wings can lift the
bearer out of the darkness and above the clouds
to heights few ever experience.

January 6th

I saw a man climb a mountain with no feet or hands and barely a stump for each arm and leg. At once I realized there was no excuse at all for me not to scale my own mountains.

January 7th

To reach a goal:
Give it your best.
Own your choices.
Ask for help.
Learn as you go.

January 8th

Chew off a little every day, because it's hard to swallow a whole pie at once.

January 9th

Nothing remains idle and thrives. Life needs a moving force to prevent the devastating effects of stagnancy. That is why life employs change.

January 10th

Weakness drives us to set goals, to try harder, to put forth more effort, to dream and wish and hope, to reach out further and down deeper, to pray earnestly, to cry mightily, to understand and empathize with valid sincerity. In truth, weakness is a catalyst for greater strength.

January 11th

When you understand that faith is God's muscle at your disposal, moving mountains doesn't seem so extraordinary.

January 12th

There are tomorrows on their way worth the struggles of today. Never give up.

January 13th

Never be intimidated by what seems ominous, for BiG is only an accumulation of many smalls.

January 14th

I know you would like to blame the world, but the fact is that life is an "up to you" thing.

January 15th

Most are unaware of their tremendous worth and boundless potential, despite possessing both.

January 16th

You can do things.
Do you know this?
Do you believe it?
You should.
It's true.
You can do great things.

January 17th

To believe in yourself is to light a spark with the potential to start a fire.

January 18th

Everything in the world that happens *to* you may be someone else's doing; I'll grant you that. But what you do with it, how you react to it, what you make of yourself in the midst of it all—that's totally you.

January 19th

It's not a dream, it's my destiny.

January 20th

Look down the road I'm traveling and you will see my goal; it's there on the path. Probably closer than it appears. Life tends to roll that way.

January 21st

Nothing can squelch your fire except turning your back on the thing that fuels it.

January 22nd

Understand that great accomplishments require great effort. If a goal is achieved without effort, it is no accomplishment but a mere happening.

January 23rd

Take it one step at a time—inarguably wise advice. And yet we all take a running leap, hoping the wind will catch us on its wings and lift us clear to the top of the beanstalk. Those few Jacks who have reached new heights in this manner inevitably wish they had taken more time to prepare for the overbearing giant who greeted them.

January 24th

In my lifetime I have witnessed far too many miracles to believe in impossibilities, and so I am officially modifying the definition.
im·pos·si·ble [im-*pos*-uh-buhl]
Old definition: Unable to be done.
New definition: Unable to be ignored until done.

January 25th

When there is not enough time to do your best, do the best you can with the time you have.

January 26th

"It isn't always true that desperate means are justified by a critical end."

—from *The Tarishe Curse*

January 27th

It turns out that the simplest choices have been far more important in the long run than I ever imagined.

January 28th

You never step backwards when you're sure of where you're going.

January 29th

Perfection may be an island out of reach, but setting your sails toward it makes for a magnificent voyage.

January 30th

The truth is, when you have little to do, you do very little. But when you have much to do, you do much. So it should make sense that by taking on more than you can handle, you accomplish more than you ever dreamed you could. And so it is.

January 31st

Don't quit.
When your latest efforts fail, don't quit. When your performance is scoffed and ridiculed, don't quit. When you're told you have no talent, don't quit. When you come in dead last, don't quit. When it seems an uphill fight to keep going, don't quit. When you can't see any possible way to achieve your goals, don't quit. When your last supporter is you alone, don't quit. When discouragement and depression seem your constant companion, don't quit. When you feel like quitting, don't quit.
Time and time again you will crave relief from the harsh fight of trying to succeed. You will falsely think that quitting will bring peace and reprieve, but alas, only regret and disappointment

await the quitter. Victory means never ever
quitting.
So don't quit.
Do not quit.

FEBRUARY

— Herensuge —
The dragon with sweet, tempting breath.

February 1st

I slay dragons at night while you sleep.
I see by the way your face contorts how they
exist in your dreams.
Willing a magic sword, I plunge into your
deepest nightmares and swing at the beasts with
all my might, dodging flames exhaled by
monsters that would eat me alive to go on
torturing the fair one I love. I see your face
relax, eyes still drowsily closed, when the mighty
dragon is slain.
It may be that my fingers rub soft circles on your
forehead as I imagine my brave fight as a knight
reclaiming your dreams. You smile under the
spell of my touch, and I am rewarded. And so,
my love, as I await the dawn, I stand ready to
slay dragons while you sleep.

February 2ⁿᵈ

It seems my heart is made of tissue paper; I wish the world would handle it more delicately.

February 3ʳᵈ

I love you for a great many reasons and despite a great many others.

February 4ᵗʰ

People search the world over looking for someone to love them, when they should be searching for someone to love.

February 5ᵗʰ

"If you were to sacrifice even a portion of yourself for the relationship, you would naturally fall in love with him. I guarantee it."

—from *Eena, The Return of a Queen*

February 6ᵗʰ

Love is donating a chunk of your life to patch up holes in the life of another.

February 7ᵗʰ

The rarest, truest beauty is visible only to the heart.

February 8ᵗʰ

The real beauty of a woman is most clearly seen in the smiles of those who interact with her.

February 9ᵗʰ

If God were to make a million lovely flowers in your image and plant them in a garden with you among them, I would still know you by your scent and by the feel of your petals and by the crazy way you lean towards my light whenever I draw near.

February 10ᵗʰ

"My knight may not wear a coat of shining armor, but his code of glowing honor will never fail to protect us both from evils far worse than any fire-breathing dragon."

—from *Smile Anyway: Quotes, Verse, & Grumblings for Every Day of the Year*

February 11th

"I love you" sounds best spoken in quiet acts of kindness.

February 12th

Love in its essence is unconditional. When conditions, exceptions, and ultimatums are cast into the mix, its purity changes. It is no longer love and should be referred to by a less-desirable name.

February 13th

Amore is love
confessed to you in haiku.
Do you love me too?

February 14th

When I ask you to be my valentine, I'm not asking you to love me. I'm simply asking you to accept tokens of my love for you.

February 15th

When you love someone, you don't care that she ate your sandwich. You only hope she found it delicious.

February 16th

Love is the ultimate no-calorie sweetener.

February 17th

Your face is engraved in my mind. I can't erase it. I don't want to. Because as much as I hate you, I love you. And I love you unforgettably.

February 18th

"Unconditional love" is a redundant expression; if it's not unconditional, then it's not love.

February 19th

Please stop. If you keep chipping off little pieces of my heart, soon there will be no heart left with which to love you.

February 20th

Maybe love isn't meant to be bliss never-ending.
Maybe love is unwavering support and
befriending.

February 21st

If you never bother to say the words, why should
anyone believe you ever felt them?

February 22nd

I hope you know I love you, not just because I
tell you so at every opportunity, but because I
show you so as often as the sun sets.

February 23rd

Love by the sweat of thy brow.
Not through whispered words of hollow sound or
lofty dreams ne'er substance bound that more
than oft do run aground. Nay, love with mighty,
blistered hands that turn the soil and carve the
land. A bearer of toil and golden band.
Be strong! A founder of the feast!
Protective knight who slays the beast!

For promises and vows aloud are naught but
wispy veneer shroud like cobwebs, frail, the airy
words and wooing fail. So work, my darling.
Toil as proof. Thy loyal heart be drained of
youth and yet beat on, incessant sound. Both feet
take root within the ground, and service be thy
kingly crown.
Love by the sweat of thy brow.

February 24th

When I first heard your voice, my heart leapt in
my chest as if it recognized you as its owner
from another lifetime.

February 25th

She laughed, and he fell in love.

February 26th

At the core of love is validation. It is what gives
love power.
For when love is given away, validation seeps in
and expands in the heart of the recipient, filling
up every empty, dark corner. It is a wonderful,
light, consuming feeling we long for, and once

found, we hope—even expect—it will forever remain. But there are times when that most precious love is revoked, and a hard scab forms over the empty hole. Though this scab is both healing and protective, it is the reason why validation from future love may not seep in so easily, no matter how wanting the heart.

February 27ᵗʰ

There is love and then there is fluff. Nothing else.

February 28ᵗʰ

"There was another longing I kept stashed in the deepest, darkest recess of my heart. It was my most compelling secret of all. Though, I suppose, it was more an empty vessel cradled by my soul wishing to someday be filled. It was my desire to belong, to be wanted, *to be loved*."

—from *Dandelions: The Disappearance of Annabelle Fancher*

February 29th

Truth is, I'm generally happiest when it's just
me. It's okay to be madly in love with yourself.

MARCH

— Guivre —

*The aggressive dragon that prowls the
countryside.*

March 1st

A dragon grows by leaps and bounds,
Like troubles mounting by the pound.

Its stature heightens day to day,
Imposing dread and deep dismay.

A paralyzing roar it gains
While from its snout hot fire rains.

It sees you cower in fear and knows
that every hour your nightmare grows.

So, lest you slay the dragon soon,
Your troubles may become your doom.

March 2nd

If you suffer lingering doubts; if the consolation you cling to is *'it will probably be okay,'* then run the other way because what you're contemplating is *not* a good choice.

March 3rd

I sat in a box
With walls on each side.
Not too tall.
Not too wide.
To think.
To ponder.
To pray.
To hide.
I sat in a box and cried.

March 4th

Sadness is the heart withdrawing to seek shelter from the pain.

Young Raccoon, for reasons real and personal, had sunk into a sorrowful mood. It wasn't just a sullen slump or a sighing sort of sadness. No. Poor Raccoon had endured one of life's harder trials and was consequently overcome with a wretched, grim, tearful type of sorrow. It wasn't long before a close friend wandered by and noticed Raccoon's dark, quiet burrow echoing a sound of sobbing. Curious and concerned, Brown Beaver invited himself in.

"Oh my, such weeping! All is not well to be sure!" Beaver hurried over and placed a hand on the shoulder of his troubled friend. "Tell me please, whatever is the matter?"

But Racoon said nothing, unless the whimpers that accompany tears can be considered a response.

"Oh dear, something must be done," determined Beaver. So he arranged a stack of wood in the hearth and lit a cozy fire.

"There now, here is a little light and comfort. Surely this will make you feel better."

But Raccoon continued to cry, rubbing at black, swollen eyes as if the light were a harsh contributor to misery.

"Oh no," sighed Beaver. "This is not good, not at all. I must go find help." With a promise to quickly return, he left Raccoon beside the fire.

Only minutes passed before Beaver stuck his head inside the warm burrow. Below him poked in a tinier head belonging to Squirrel.

"Oh dear, oh dear, you're right! This is a miserable sight!"

Squirrel hurried into the room and proceeded to remove a handful of nuts stored in his cheeks. He then tossed them into a pan over the smoldering fire built by Beaver. Soon, the room was saturated with the rich, buttery smell of roasted nuts.

"Here you are, Raccoon," said Squirrel, shaking the nuts onto a plate. "Some comfort food will certainly make you feel better. Try one."

Raccoon didn't even glance at the offered plate but continued to cry and sniffle as if the fragrant smell were an enhancer of sadness. Squirrel looked at Beaver. Both were clueless as to what to do.

"We must go find someone who can help," they decided.

As quick as a wink the pair left and returned with Black Cat who took a minute to size up the situation. She then confidently declared, "We must dry up these tears, for no one can eat and be happy when soaked in tears!"

With that thought, the three friends wiped at Raccoon's wet fur, sopping up handkerchiefs in the process. Black Cat even went so far as to purr a quiet, relaxing chord while licking at the glistening fur around Raccoon's eyes, and yet the tears continued to spill, replacing those washed away.

"Well, this most certainly is not working," Cat finally admitted, lamentably swooshing her tail. Beaver and Squirrel readily agreed. "We must go find someone who can help!"

They hardly stepped outside when the slender form of Corn Snake appeared in the road and slithered over to them. Snake was informed as to Raccoon's sorry state and came up with a fine idea.

"The poor dear simply needs some hugs and kisses. A bit of affection will dry up those unhappy tears."

Agreeing it was worth a try, the four turned right around to enter the burrow and encircle Raccoon, administering snug hugs and tender kisses. Snake gave an especially tight hug, but it had no effect at all on Raccoon's woeful weeping. Even a ticklish kiss from a forked tongue received no favorable response. The four friends were beginning to feel a bit glum themselves when Calandra Lark came flittering into the burrow.

"Tweet, tweet, tweet! Whatever is the matter?"

"Oh dear, Calandra, just look! Raccoon is extremely sad. Yet as hard as we have tried, our efforts have failed to stop the tears."

"Is that all?" Calandra Lark chirped, perching on the fireplace mantle. "'Tis nothing a happy song can't remedy."

Puffing out her feathery chest to convey a mountain of confidence, the little bird began to chirp a bright and lively tune. Calandra twittered and tweeted and even trilled many a string of notes, but the cheerier the tune, the more Raccoon appeared to cry. At long last, Miss Lark ceased singing.

"Oh what is to be done?" she sighed. "There must be someone who can help!" No sooner had she said the words then a high-pitched squeal of laughter carried from outside. Swinging down from a tree into the warm, crowded burrow, Monkey addressed a group of surprised onlookers.

"Did I hear that someone is in need of my help?"

"Oh yes, indeed!" the five agreed simultaneously. "Look here! Raccoon is so sad, and yet nothing we have done has relieved the weeping!"

Monkey laughed aloud again, not meaning to be insensitive. "Eee, eee, eee! Do not worry, for I will cheer up our good friend in an instant!"

Monkey crossed the room on feet and hands to stand directly before the saddest of souls. He then delved into chipper chatter, telling jokes, answering his own riddles, and laughing at his own humorous stories. At last, he attempted only calm words of comfort because Raccoon continued to cry, making pitiable noises as if the jollity was anguish to bear. Needless to say, nothing worked to halt the tears.

"Oh me, oh my! Poor, poor, poor Raccoon!" the company cried, succumbing to a measure of grief and sorrow themselves. "Please, tell us— whatever is the matter with you?" But Raccoon shrank into a tighter ball, withdrawing while giving them no answer.

Overwhelmed with concern, the six good friends stepped outside Raccoon's burrow to discuss the problem, hoping to hit upon a solution. They were running short of ideas. Debating whether or not to render the weeper unconscious, a strong voice of objection cut them off. Every head turned to see Red Fox step out of the underbrush.

"Oh, Fox, if not this, then what should we do? For Raccoon has been crying inconsolably for hours! We have tried light and warmth, tempting food, wiping away tears, hugs and affection, cheerful songs, and kind words of comfort. None of it has had any effect on Raccoon's dreadful sadness!"

Red Fox walked up to the burrow entrance on quiet paws, but before ducking inside he turned and voiced an idea no one else had possessed the sense to think up. For it seemed to them rather senseless.

"Sadness is like a cloud in the sky; it exists out of grasp. Therefore, the only option is to let sadness be sad until it is not."

Curious as to what Red Fox intended to do, the others followed him inside. There, he took a seat beside Raccoon and waited. He did nothing but sit. Nothing at all.

Confused—yet lacking a better idea—Beaver, Squirrel, Black Cat, Corn Snake, Calandra Lark, and Monkey all settled inside Raccoon's burrow and likewise did nothing. The house remained quiet for hours upon hours as weeping, sniveling, and the occasional sigh carried over the sound of a crackling fire kept alive by Beaver.

Time passed.

Some nodded off for a brief spell, but no one left the room or made any attempt to keep sadness from being sad—as Fox had wisely declared.

Eventually and at long last, the gloomy cloud dissipated. All eyes turned to Raccoon, realizing that what had seemed like inconsolable grief had somehow transformed. Raccoon sat up and looked around, exchanging a small smile with each and every sympathetic face.

"Thank you, my friends."

"Thank you for what?" someone asked, though others certainly wondered. For while Raccoon had wept a river of tears, they had done nothing but sit as still and noiseless as tree stumps.

Squeezing paws with Red Fox, Raccoon softly said, "Thank you for giving me time."

That's when they understood. More often than not, the only thing that can lift the heavy fog of sorrow is time.

March 6th

Sadness is like sandpaper; it rubs at our sharper edges, softening and humbling us, making us ready for a coat of compassion.

March 7th

To be a rainbow in someone's cloud is commendable, but I prefer to be the rain because it dampens cheeks and washes away tears.

March 8th

I think in the heart of every human being there burns an ember of hope that warmly entices us to believe everything will eventually come together into one perfect day, and that potentially the hours in this day will stretch on indefinitely. And so we live our lives in hopeful anticipation, dreaming and praying to reach this wondrous day, while in the process we miss out on the anxious affair that life truly is. Life is not perfection; it is everything else. We must taste and experience heartaches and trials in order to feel the genuine joy that comes from enduring them well. We then move on, wiser and more capable of charity—this being pure love and the reason for life's trials altogether.

March 9th

God cries for us in the same way we cry for others. His tears most often spill over for the pain and suffering caused from the mortal misuse of a gift called agency. He will not revoke the gift. It was promised to us for the duration of our time on Earth. But He will hold each one of us accountable in the end for how we applied this power of agency.

March 10th

Every heart has a layer of sadness, whether deeply buried or covering the surface for all to see.

March 11th

How frustrating to think you can be lost to yourself. And yet how often it is that a stranger stares back at you from the mirror. Maybe in truth we never see ourselves as clearly as the thousands of eyes that daily take us in.

March 12th

Too often we let others stamp a price tag on us and we accept their appraisal of our worth, forgetting we are in fact priceless.

March 13th

If I expect nothing of you, it will be far easier to forgive your offenses than if I place my whole world in your hands.

March 14th

The wind is made of haunting souls
that moan and groan
in whistles and whispers.
This ghostly choir chills the breeze
and orchestrates a rise of goose bumps
on my skin.

March 15th

Every single voice—no matter how soft the peep—longs to be heard.

March 16th

It's simply this:
the Irish kiss,
a snog o' bliss,
be blessed luck
from any miss.

March 17th

Be sure to wear green
on March seventeen,
or else Irish leprechauns
pinch your bones clean!

March 18th

Smile wide to receive many smiles in return. But
if you want a good laugh, smirk like a wicked
imp and watch the range of expressions you're
flashed.

March 19th

Sunshine warms us, as do smiles—which makes
me think that smiles are sunbeams reflected off
our teeth.

March 20th

Laugh and smile for no reason at all. Giggle
grins are a magnet for happiness.

March 21ˢᵗ

Sometimes the craziest laugh in the world is the
one that will save your sanity.

March 22ⁿᵈ

A smile is a light that sets your inner self aglow,
letting others know you're home.

March 23ʳᵈ

My soul, I've found, has puppet strings
to make me droop or give me wings.
And music is the puppeteer
that turns my ear to hear.

March 24ᵗʰ

Music is happiness with a steady pulse.

March 25ᵗʰ

Life is music to which you choreograph your
own dance.

March 26th

Sound.
Noise
the air employs.
Melodies sweet.
Tweet, tweet, tweet.
Soft. Loud.
A roaring crowd.
Cluck. Caw. Crow.
Tet, tet. Tis, tis.
Guttural growl.
Harrowing howl.
Drip, drip, drip.
Tap, tap, tap.
Moan and groan.
Endless drone.
Ding, dang, dong.
A church bell song.
Vibrations in my ear
to hear.
Sound.

March 27th

As sunlight is for flowers, and sustenance for the
mortal shell, music is for the human soul.

March 28th

Happiness is never in a rush. If you move too
fast, you leave it behind.

March 29th

Alas, impatience is but another form of
unhappiness. It is true, it is true. I have never
met a happy impatient person.

March 30th

Impatience is racing at misery full speed.

March 31st

How easy it is to slip.
How hard it is to climb.
How wise it is to keep in step
And never fall behind.

APRIL

— Naga —
The first dragon, divine and benevolent.

April 1st

Easter is the miracle of transformation as seen in the change of seasons, in the maturation of mortal persons, and in the resurrection of souls.

April 2nd

On Easter we wrap up pretty, little decorated eggs symbolizing life and renewal. We do this because of the intangibility of a promised gift, which is the eventual resurrection of the body, restored to its finest forever state. Easter celebrates life and the idea of its eternal value, most notably the life of the gift-giver who demands nothing in return. He is your Lord and Savior, Jesus Christ.

April 3ʳᵈ

With the best of intentions, you toss me a
lifeline. Failing to see how a piece of rope will
do me any good, I ignore it and drown.

April 4ᵗʰ

In the darkest night the sun may seem like an
extinguished match or an ember drowned by rain.

A light forever lost.

The cold world grows steadily colder and shrinks
like the abused, closing in on all sides. Laughter,
smiles, the glimmer of dancing eyes, and all else
indicative of human brightness is gone. Colors
leeched from everything leave shadows and
emotion dull-gray in their absence.
Time is a void. A moment feels eternal.
Hope does not blossom in the darkness but
withers fast, starving for what only the sun can
offer. As its petals turn to dust, fear blows in and
sweeps the remnants away. The soul succumbs
by degrees to nightmares emboldened by the
dead of night.

All is lost! All is lost! The wretched sun,
repulsed by our nothingness, has abandoned the
lives in its care!

And then the eyes open wide, seeing mountains
take shape on the horizon.

April 5th

Sympathy is imagining the pain. Empathy is
having suffered through it first.

April 6th

We all suffer ills at the hands of others; however,
reactions to these injustices differ like night and
day. Many seek to punish the world for their
suffering, while some work hard to save the
world from experiencing similar grief.

April 7th

Empathy is a hand thick with scars offering you a
bandage.

April 8th

I scared a little porcupine
and caught a quill in my behind.
It hurt so badly in my tail,
but tugging on it made me yell.

The porcupine was still around,
so I complained. He simply frowned
and said, "Stop whining! Look and see
how many quills are stuck on me!"

April 9th

It's easy to offer advice on trials that have caused
you to stumble. It's harder to talk about those
that have knocked you flat.

April 10th

Giving advice is like seeing an elephant in
someone's path and suggesting they remove it.
Heeding advice requires forcing the elephant to
budge. Huge difference.

April 11th

Raindrops fall from clouds of gray.
The fragile flowers grow.
Teardrops seem all I can say.
They speak of endless woe.
Your fingers wipe my grief away.
A seed of love you sow.
A hardened heart reverts to clay.
You mold my love just so.

April 12th

The soft heart is not a thing to harden but a treasure to protect. For soft hearts extend mercy, compassion, refuge, and God's redemption to the world.

April 13th

People think kindness is a soft, weak, submissive influence when in reality it is the most potent, persuasive force in existence.

April 14th

Forgiveness is kindness regardless.

April 15th

Numerous times throughout history, a single person has made a tremendous impact on the world. I don't know why anyone would think that can't still happen.

April 16th

Kindness is going out of your way to perform favors regarded as wonderful by the recipient.

April 17th

If kindness is beauty, patience is disarming elegance.

April 18th

Beauty is a behavior. As is ugliness.

April 19th

Even if the grass *is* greener on the other side of the fence, keep to your own side; it's where you belong. There you can plant your own grass and tend to it.

April 20th

"Time passes.....and a billion lives are affected in ways we'll never know."

—from *Dandelions: The Disappearance of Annabelle Fancher*

April 21st

One day a week I seek to rest
        from earthly toil and sorrow.
Revitalized, I find the strength
        to battle new tomorrows.

April 22nd

Observe the Lord's Day as he would have you, and perhaps He will observe your days as you would have Him.

April 23rd

Man is dust.
    Rue is rain.
        Life is mud.

April 24th

Forgiving yourself can prove as difficult as
licking a scab off your elbow.

April 25th

Have you honestly pondered your individual
worth? Consider every lower life form in the
world—the animals, plants, fouls and fishes.
Consider the land forms and numerous earthly
wonders. Consider the countless worlds beyond
this planet as well as their stars and galaxies.
And then consider yourself. Of all God's
creations, you were formed in his image,
resembling the likeness of a God. That's
something to think about.

April 26th

If I were to sit on the ocean floor and look
toward the sky,
I might see a whale or electric eel or octopus pass
by.

And if I decided to jump straight up and reach
with open arms,

I might feel the pleasure of ocean flight propel
me 'mid their swarms.

But if I were seated upon the shore and looking
toward the stars,
I might see a comet or falling star near Mercury
or Mars.

Then if I decided to jump straight up and reach
with open hands,
I might feel despair when my feet refused to
leave the shoreline sand.

And so I return to the ocean depths where
swimming creatures fly,
For there I can soar with the whales and fish that
daily touch the sky.

April 27th

I cast my eyes out to the sea
And gaze at all eternity.
until forever turns to night.
My eyes then lift to catch starlight.

April 28th

Sometimes a problem isn't really a problem but the solution in disguise.

April 29th

It is a great mystery to me how the problems of others seem like simple arithmetic while my own appear as complicated as a calculus equation.

April 30th

"Such a nasty bruise," he says, staring straight into my eyes. I am stunned he can see it. Delicate to the touch and tender on every side, the bruise is deeper than days. My hand automatically moves to my chest.

Science taught me with valid assurance that my heart was fixed in my rib cage, but life has since shown me otherwise. My heart in fact dangles from a tangle of strings. The ends are grasped tight by numerous people who yank and release, having caused many painful bruises over time. I cry because they are invisible to most.

"Such a nasty bruise," he repeats, tugging on my poor heart.

His kind eyes fall away from mine as I feel a squeeze on my arm. He twists it enough to show me a small, round patch of purple surrounded by a sickly yellowish corona.

"Oh. My elbow." I let the air exhale from my lungs. Another bruise forms where my heart has hit the floor. It is jerked up again.

"Can I do anything for you?" I see in his eyes the mirror image of a finger—his finger—wrapped in one of the dangling strings. He tugs and I feel it.

"No," I reply to his question. But it is a lie. There is something he could do, along with all who grasp a portion of the web entangling my heart. I wish they would mercifully let go.

MAY

May 1st

If I could have one friend,
just one in all the world,
I know that I would not seek out
a boy or pretty girl.

The friend I'd dare to choose
to stand by me each day
would be a dragon fierce enough
to scare the world away.

May 2nd

If you often feel alone, ignored, or forgotten,
think about this: closing the door and locking
yourself in won't change anything—literally and
figuratively.

May 3rd

Friends are the real superheroes. They battle our worst enemies—loneliness, grief, anxiety, depression, fear, and doubt—every time they come around.

May 4th

Friends are the artists who paint happy lips on your face.

May 5th

Rather than critique people, try admiring God's creative handiwork.

May 6th

Hatred is prevalent on this earth because it requires no real effort, unlike the investment it takes to genuinely understand a person.

May 7ᵗʰ

We live that we might have experience; that through it we might gain wisdom, compassion, faith, and inner strength.

May 8ᵗʰ

Heaven's currency is friendship.

May 9ᵗʰ

I never realized how much you meant to me until someone spoke your name and an irrepressible, goofy grin stretched my lips.

May 10ᵗʰ

On a grim and dismal day that shattered my last ounce of confidence, I broke down and whimpered, "I'm awful and hideous and incompetent and boring and utterly useless." And then you grinned at me and said, "That's okay."

May 11th

"I love you" means I want you to be happy.

May 12th

Mothers
Offer
Their
Hearts as an
Eternal
Resting
Spot

May 13th

I never knew what Mother knowed,
Like how a thread and needle sewed,
And how a kiss healed boo-boos fast.
Why family knots were made to last.

I never knew how Mother saw
A caring man in angry pa,
A smile beneath the teary gloom,
A game inside a messy room.

I never knowed what Mother knew,
Like how to smile when days were blue,

And how to laugh for laughter's sake,
While giving up her slice of cake.

I never saw what Mother see'd
Like honor pulling garden weeds,
Or deep confessions in a look,
And hope alive in storybooks.

I never knew how Mother knowed
To hand out carrots when it snowed,
And why hot cocoa liked the rain,
While naptime kept a person sane.

For mother knowed and see'd it all.
A winner in a strike-out ball.
A "yes, please" in a shoulder shrug.
A "love you mostest" in a hug.

Perhaps, someday, I'll come to know
What Mother saw and knowed as so.
Like how "I'm right" can be all wrong,
And why the night requires a song.

But of the things I learned and knew
I never doubted one thing true.
My mother made it crystal clear,
she knowed and loved me ever dear.

May 14th

You breathe.
You feel.
You see,
and hear,
and smell,
and taste,
and think,
and move,
and laugh,
and weep,
and heal,
and dance,
and sing,
and love.
Thank your mother.

May 15th

"One of the strongest loves I've ever witnessed is
the love a mother has for her child."

—from *Eena, The Return of a Queen*

May 16th

My mother does not own my hands, though she
works hard to train them.
My mother does not own my eyes, though she
frequently directs their focus.
My mother does not own my mind, though she
yields great influence upon it.
My heart, however, she owns completely, for it
was hers the day I was born.

May 17th

Things that remind me of Mother are these:
the truth 'mid deception, a warm summer breeze,
the calm within chaos, a stitch in a rip,
a comforting blanket, the smile on her lip,
an ocean of love in a heart big as whales,
the morals in everyday stories she tells,
a wink amid laughter, the wisdom in books,
the peace in humility, beauty in looks,
the light and the life in a ray of the sun,
the hard work accomplished disguised as pure
fun,
concern in a handclasp, encouragement too,
the hope in a clear morning sky azure blue,
the power in prayers uttered soft and sincere,
the faith in a promise, and joy in a tear.

These things all attest to the wonder and grace
of my precious mother, none else could replace.

May 18th

In one way or another,
you owe your life to Mother.

May 19th

Patience isn't simply waiting, it is caring enough
about the situation and those involved to remain
calm and courteous throughout the wait.

May 20th

Extraordinary power exists in a trial of patience.
Few endure their trials well enough to discover
this.

May 21st

Patience is real self-mastery.

May 22nd

Progressing at a snail's pace is still progress, and slow progress is better than no progress. Never be stagnant, and never give up.

May 23rd

Patience is seeing each step as a journey rather than seeing a journey as a thousand steps.

May 24th

"Despair is not for the living but for those unable to rise and continue; they are the only souls with a right to it. It is an end where breath and strength and will have vanished, leaving no way to persevere. To sink into the abyss that is despair is to suffer an existence far worse than death; therefore, cling to its enemy, our ally— hope. For life goes on, and we must not live in despair. We must not."

—from *Eena, The Two Sisters*

May 25th

Pray as if you are fully aware that the intricate
timing and rotation of every celestial entity in the
universe—including the coming and going of
innumerable, precious life forms—does not rest
in your tiny, mortal hands.

May 26th

A word of consolation
may sweetly touch the ear.
Now and then a quiet song
will clear the mind of fear.

A simple act of kindness
can ease a load of care.
Stories told in memory
diminish all despair.

A whispered prayer of comfort
draws angel arms around.
Counting blessings, great and small,
helps gratitude abound.

These acts, all sympathetic,
will kindly play their part.
But seldom do they dry the tears
shed mutely in the heart.

May 27th

It is important that we remember.
It is vital we do more than *just* remember.

May 28th

On this day, take time to remember those who
have fallen. But on every day after, do more; put
the freedoms they died for to greater and nobler
uses.

May 29th

Remembering our loved ones is breathing life
into their fading images, that we might once
more see their faces and pass along a tearful "I
miss you."

May 30th

When we all part from this life and gather on the
other side, the only thing each of us will have to
share is his own story.

May 31ˢᵗ

Death lurks in the shadows, just out of view.
Now and then I see his reaching hand, uncertain
of the blurry image that passes before my eyes,
but conscious of the crippling influence of his
touch.
Some say Death rears an ugly head, so hideous a
view the beholder can scarcely gasp their last
breath. Others call him beautiful, a sweet relief
to look upon. But these are rumors babbled by
the unknowing. For Death is like the gorgon,
Medusa, who when perceived, turns the body to
stone.
Those who know Death take the knowledge of
his shadowed face with them to wherever it is he
leads our dearly departed by the hand. All who
are left behind must wait their turn to glance into
the eyes of the one who will close our mouths
forever.

JUNE

June 1st

It may seem like the dragons tormenting you are bigger and fiercer than those lurking in your neighbor's yard, but this is an illusion. We all face mighty dragons at home in some form.

June 2nd

Problems are never as difficult as when they are your own.

June 3rd

It isn't so much life's problems that challenge us but the emotional turbulence stirred up while trying to deal with them. People possessing the gift of emotional detachment are lucky in that their personal problems seem far less problematic.

June 4th

If life is a stage and you are your own agent, then don't hesitate to play the character you wish to play.

June 5th

Life is a fierce duel with emotions and a slow war with psychology.

June 6th

A box sits empty,
wanting to hold and protect.
Hollow tears it cries.

June 7th

Mind what you say, but mind more closely what you do. For though children close their ears to you, their eyes remain wide open.

June 8th

Children rarely follow parental advice unless it is acted out repeatedly. It's called being an example.

June 9th

Effective parenting requires being the grown up version of what you want your children to be. Why? Because example is the most compelling superpower.

June 10th

I am but the reflection in your eyes, the effect of your expressions, and the sum of your praise and criticism.

June 11th

Validate my existence with your words and I will speak to you all the day long.

June 12ᵗʰ

"To encourage me is to believe in me,
which gives me the power to defeat dragons."

—from *Smile Anyway: Quotes, Verse, & Grumblings
for Every Day of the Year*

June 13ᵗʰ

There should ne'er be a time
When a duty or dime
Doth outshine
The importance of family.

June 14ᵗʰ

I always envisioned myself as traveling the ocean
of life in a rowboat where my mother was one
oar and my father, the other. Having two good,
solid oars made rowing much easier.

June 15ᵗʰ

The best fathers have the softest, sweetest hearts.
In other words, great dads are real
marshmallows.

June 16th

Father always said that money doesn't grow on trees. Well, time doesn't grow on trees either.

June 17th

Fathers
Are
The
Humble
Everyday
Real
Servicemen

June 18th

A great father is one whose children look up to him rather than away from him.

June 19th

Children harbor a great many doubts and sorrows that could be eased by a loving hug from a parent.

June 20th

I may deserve your disappointment as well as a lecture and strict discipline, but what I need is your understanding, your guidance, and your unconditional love.

June 21st

A hero is a person who, without a second thought, simply does the right thing because his conscience cannot live with any other choice.

June 22nd

Heroes don't have the need to be known as heroes, they just do what heroes do because it is right and it must be done.

June 23rd

Meanness is a monster that usurps your self-control because you cowardly allow it to conquer you.

June 24th

Barking at people earns their respect about as effectively as staring into the sun improves your vision.

June 25th

Learn to brush off criticism as easily as you brush aside hollow compliments.

June 26th

You are mistaken; he is not a gentleman but a sir. Just a sir. For a gentleman is grander and a rare acquaintance.

June 27th

A gentleman will
Never allow a lady
To feel less than grand.

June 28th

Integrity is more than truth and honesty; integrity is an unshackled mind, a happy heart, and a light spirit. Integrity is inner peace with a clear, clean conscience. Integrity is self-respect, honor, and credibility. Integrity is healthy and unfettering, and it is worth defending.

June 29th

When gossip starts, be deaf.

June 30th

Little Gracie Gubler was eight. She was a striking sight with her lava-red hair that hung as curly as a piglet's tail and the sprinkling of cinnamon freckles on her nose and cheeks and fingers and toes. When she stood in place, it was with both feet apart, hands on her hips, shoulders square, chin high, lips grinning as if she were the most remarkable child in a school where nearly every other student towered over her. The truth is, Gracie's confidence and pluck overflowed more than most. And it happened that these qualities—made manifest in her demeanor and countenance—were hard not to stare at.

Now, this freckle-faced, sprightly child had been born with a small frame and small ears that were somehow well-tuned to surrounding chit-chat. And Gracie Gubler had no qualms about joining in on a transpiring conversation if the topic proved of interest to her. In fact, she did so quite often. On one tulip-blooming spring day she happened to overhear Jeffrey Turner and Dylan Ewing gossiping about Mr. Quilter's bald head—a head that had been covered with blond fuzz just a week ago. It was the last time they had seen their math teacher until he walked into school that morning without his hair. Jeffrey and Dylan were discussing Mr. Quilter as if they were piecing together a puzzle that would reveal the whole story; never mind if there existed any amount of truth to it.

"I heard that he was away on family business."

"That's what adults call it when it's serious."

"Yeah, like when someone dies."

"Or when they're going to die….like from a disease."

"Like cancer."

"Yeah. You know, they shave your head bald if you get cancer."

"No they don't; your hair falls out on its own. That's what cancer does. That's how they know you have it."

"Well, it amounts to the same thing."

"Not really."

"Yeah, really. And either way your head ends out bald, just like Mr. Quilter."

77

"Poor guy's probably real sick. No wonder he needed a week off."

"Yeah. I bet he doesn't even know that when your hair falls out it's the worst kind of cancer. He'll probably be dead in another week."

"Or sooner." The boys sighed a dismal sigh in concert. About that time, Gracie Gubler joined in their conversation.

"Do you two know what you're talking about?" she asked. "Did Mr. Quilter tell you he was sick?"

Dylan and Jeffrey exchanged a guarded glance before answering. "Well, no, not exactly, but he didn't have to say anything. He missed a week of school and came back with no hair…"

"And he's acting really tired. It's obvious he's seriously sick."

"Yeah, and only cancer takes all your hair that fast."

Gracie pursed her lips together and placed both hands on her hips before swiveling about and marching directly to the school's math room. There she found Mr. Quilter sitting at his desk, his bald head lowered into his hands. He did look tired. The classroom was empty; all the kids were outside on the playground.

Gracie interrupted the math teacher by clearing her voice. When he looked up, she asked him a simple question.

"Mr. Quilter, why is your head bald?"

After flashing a humored smile, he proceeded to explain how he had flown home to attend the funeral of his grandfather the prior week, and during that time he had been invited to play on his brother's basketball team. Mr. Quilter had eagerly agreed, being tall and athletic and quite fond of the game. He had been less eager to agree to shaving his head in order to look like the other team players who took great pride in reflecting through appearances their team name—the Bald Eagles. However, a little guilt-ridden convincing by his brother had done the trick. Mr. Quilter flashed a wry smile as he rubbed his head and told Gracie, "It does make for faster showers in the morning."

Little Gracie told her math teacher that she thought he looked fine with a bald head. Then she marched outside to report the truth to Jeffrey and Dylan who had already convinced a dozen surrounding children that they would soon be getting a new math teacher. Gracie stated that it was not so.

Later that day, outside the local grocery store where a troop of girl scouts was selling mint crèmes and coconut clusters and chunky chocolate cookies, Gracie was exiting the store behind her mother who stopped to purchase three boxes of mint crèmes, supporting the troop that her friend, Karin Summers, happened to direct as a parent volunteer. Both adults watched a neighbor lady, Miss Tyra Darling, walk out of the store carrying a case of beer in either hand. They began to talk in loud whispers, easily overheard by curious, young ears.

"That's four cases this week. I saw Tyra purchase two cases a couple days ago."

"Really? I say, that's an awful lot of beer for a single woman who lives alone."

"She's got an obvious drinking problem. Beverly, who lives right next door to Tyra, told me no one ever comes over to that lonely house. Tyra never throws any parties or anything. Not that Beverly wants any loud, drunken partiers carrying on next door."

"No, no, I'm sure she doesn't want that. She would have to call the cops on something like that."

"The woman is just a serious alcoholic. No doubt she'll die from a bad liver—young and miserably alone."

"What a tragedy. I don't understand why people do stuff like that to themselves."

During this conversation, every girl scout from Hannah Pepper to Hallie Nogues had their ears perked, listening. Gracie Gubler, alone, spun about and marched toward the silver sedan in which Tyra Darling had deposited her two cases of beer. The woman was just opening the driver's seat door when a chipper "excuse me" stopped her. Gracie went to stand directly under Tyra's nose and looked up to ask a simple question.

"Miss Darling, are you going to drink all of those beers yourself?"

The shocked recipient of the question put a hand to her heart, and her cheeks flushed red. She laughed at the thought. "Oh dear, dear, no, no!" She then leaned forward and explained to little Gracie that her hobby and passion was gardening. Every spring and summer she tended to a half an acre of garden behind her house which included rare flowers mixed with all sorts of herbs, fruits, and vegetables. The beer was used as bait in homemade bowl-traps that effectively lured and killed slugs, snails, and earwigs. She also sprayed the trees and bushes with beer because it attracted the most beautiful butterflies to her garden. Tyra laughed again and skewed her eyebrows. "I don't even like the taste of beer," she said. "But I will admit, I do mix up a pretty good beer batter when I'm in the mood for a fish fry."

After accepting Miss Darling's invitation to drop by at a later date and visit the beer-fertilized garden, Little Gracie Gubler marched back to report the truth to her mother and Karin (as well

81

as the eavesdropping girl scouts.) The adults stared silently at Gracie for a few stunned moments.

"Huh, that's good to know."

"Yeah. I wonder if I could get her beer batter recipe."

The next day at school, freckle-faced Gracie was in the library checking out a fairytale storybook about Dimearians—people born with moth-type wings on their backs. She cocked an ear when she overheard Russ Montgomery whispering (partly because he was in a library and partly because he was gossiping) about LeiAnn Jones, a new girl from Wisconsin who had joined their class two weeks prior. She had proven to be a quiet sort and had checked out five thick books after receiving special permission from the librarian.

"She's a snot, I tell you. Thinks she's smarter and better than the rest of us. I bet she doesn't even read those books. Just showing off, hoping the rest of us will think Wisconsin grows brainiacs like it grows cheese."

"I'm pretty sure they don't *grow* cheese..." someone started to say.

"You know what I mean. That LeiAnn girl is so big-headed, she won't even say 'how d'ya do' to anyone. Has she talked to you? 'Cause she hasn't said one word to me."

"Nuh-uh."

"Nope."

"Not one word."

"And have you said one word to her?"

The question took the other kids by surprise, in part because it was voiced louder than appropriate for a library setting, but mostly because the speaker had not been included in the conversation. Gracie Gubler ran her probing eyes over every kid huddled about the reading table. Then she turned and headed to a corner of the library where LeiAnn Jones was sitting by herself with a pile of books on her lap. She had one cracked open hiding her face. It took LeiAnn a moment to lower the book when she heard someone address her by name. As soon as Gracie could see the blue of LeiAnn's eyes, she asked a simple question.

"Why don't you join the rest of the class at the reading table?"

LeiAnn glanced in the direction of the other kids who were staring with tight eyes at Gracie's back. The new girl swallowed hard, and then timidly explained that she felt uncomfortable. No one had invited her to sit with them, and she didn't want to assume they would welcome her. Shrugging it off, she told the inquisitive red-head that she was fine—"I have my books." LeiAnn then confessed, "I'm not very good at making new friends."

After chatting with LeiAnn Jones, finding that they had a common love for fantasy books, Gracie marched back to the reading table to report the truth to Russ Montgomery and the other children, after which a few of them decided to go introduce themselves to the new girl.

And so it was with Gracie. Whenever she heard someone speak a word of assuming gossip, she was quick to learn and share the truth. Thus, Bobby Black learned that he had not been callously dumped by Darin Caraway as a best friend; the birthday invitation had been mailed by his mother to the wrong address. Elizabeth Bifano learned that Kimmy Jackson did in fact adore her daisy-yellow dress, even though Kimmy's least favorite color in the world was yellow. Madelyn Jenks learned that their school teacher did not own a jar where he kept the names of bad students he meant to feed to the alligators at the end of the school year. And Mindi Bergeson learned that Scarlet Elliott's unfortunate case of acne was not the result of kissing frogs in the pond on the Elliot's farm. Therefore, when anyone saw the little freckle-faced redhead marching near, they would check their conversation—because if their comments weren't the verified truth, it was foolish business to gossip in front of Gracie Gubler.

JULY

— Lotan —
The fugitive serpent with seven heads.

July 1ˢᵗ

Courage isn't being a dragon. Neither is it
behaving like a dragon. Nor is it taking up arms
to fight and defeat dragons. Courage is being a
lamb standing with poise among dragons.

July 2ⁿᵈ

Courage doesn't defeat fear or erase fear or
adjust to fear. Courage acts, plain and simple, in
the midst of fear.

July 3ʳᵈ

Do you feel that? It is a calm shift in the wind.
Do you hear that? It is a soft whisper of hope.
Do you see that? It is the divine hand of
guidance, mercifully extended to aid our good
fight.

July 4th

"Ma'am," he said, reaching for the door. He held it open, his posture as erect and sturdy as a pole.

I eyed the man's uniform, the pins and badges that signified his military rank and position. At that moment I felt opposing forces wash over me, clashing internally like a cold and warm front meeting in the air.

At first I was hit by a burning sense of respect and gratitude. How privileged a person I was to have this soldier unbar the way for me, maintaining a clear path that I might advance unhindered. The symbolism marked by his actions did strike me with remarkable intensity. How many virtual doors would be shut in my face if not for dutiful soldiers like him?

As I went to step forward, my feet nearly faltered as if they felt unworthy. It was I who ought to be holding open the door for this gentleman—this representative of great heroes present and past who did fight and sacrifice and continue to do so to keep doors open, paths free and clear for all of humanity.

I moved through the entrance and thanked him.

"Yes, ma'am," he said.

How strange that I should feel such pride while passing through his open door.

July 5th

Mad fearlessness is not courage. The only requirement for courage is a good heart.

July 6th

If you think the most courageous and difficult thing you can do is stubbornly stand your ground, try graciously giving in.

July 7th

You tell me that yes, I can do it. I know.
And I may do it, if I so choose.
You tell me that no, I cannot. I say, Oh?
I shall do it, since you refuse!

July 8th

Stubbornness is surely just taut-jawed, clenched-fisted madness.

July 9ᵗʰ

Stubbornness is a weapon.
People tend to draw it out when a sensitive part
of their identity is threatened—be it dignity,
honor, pride, desires, etc. If loaded with
righteous resolve, stubbornness can assist in
overcoming obstacles and achieving great feats;
however, more often than not it is loaded with
anger, used as a means of destruction for both the
possessor and those whom he turns his weapon
upon. It is best utilized by wise individuals who
are able to dispassionately perceive if their
stubbornness will accomplish good, or if it
should be put away and replaced by a humble
substitute to spare the lives of everyone affected.

July 10ᵗʰ

The most powerful and courageous heroes I
know are those who bite their tongues when
justification, validation, temptation, or vengeance
would have them strike with truthful, hurtful
words.

July 11th

My favorite words in the world are these:
"what" and *"if"* in conjunction.
They question curiosities
in simple form and function.
"What" is a query of broadest scope.
"If" is wonder that fuels all hope.
Together they lasso the mind like rope, and spur
the wildest deductions!

July 12th

What if stars were the glimmering tears of a
giant, welling in his cheeks, waiting to fall at the
first tender stroke of emotion? What if the moon
were a wide-open eye gazing down on our tiny,
little world and its tiny, little inhabitants as they
rush to and fro in pursuit of tiny, little dreams?
What if the sun were the glowing heart of a great
beast, pumping hot blood to keep him alive while
providing warmth for our pitiful world? Ahhh,
imagination; it is a wondrous thing!

July 13th

An inexhaustible imagination is the fountain of
youth.

91

July 14th

"The truth is that few know the truth."

—from *Secrets of a Noble Key Keeper*

July 15th

What if dragons breathed bubbles
and purred when they cuddled
and giggled at chivalrous knights for their
troubles?

What if dragons felt soft,
having scales made of cloth,
and they moved rather slow like a brown-
throated sloth?

What if dragons were shy
and did easily cry
when confronted by characters callous and sly?

What if dragons did good
but were misunderstood
so men mercilessly slew the beasts right where
they stood?

What if dragons aren't missed

because there is no list
of extinct types of quarry that now don't exist?

July 16th

I used to play in the hot July wind and
imagine it was dragon's breath singeing my skin.
I would clamber up the hill behind our home as if
I were a knight intent on hunting down and
slaying the beast. For I would try to rouse it by
making a ruckus as loud and annoying as a
lonely pup. But no dragon responded to my
verbal challenges, and I was never lucky enough
to stumble upon any large, fire-breathing animal.
Not until the day I turned ten.

That day was not unlike other hot and windy
July afternoons when I scrambled up the green
hill that blocked faraway scenery from the
windows of our house. And like every other
time, I brandished my invisible sword, imagining
it glistening in the sunlight, bejeweled at the hilt
with priceless sapphires and rubies. I swore
aloud to slay the dragon whose hot breath was
the source of the July winds—or so it seemed in
a boy's creative mind—and hustled with great
energy and determination up the rocky terrain.

I had climbed only partway when the toe of
my shoe managed to lodge itself beneath the

edge of a smooth, pearly rock. I nearly fell over and would surely have dropped my treasured sword had it actually been made from physical substance. But it remained in my hand and, finding my shoe unable to slide out from beneath the pale stone, I pretended to jab at it with the tip of my sword as if this poking attack would surely persuade whatever had taken such a fast hold to release me. For a short period of time I entertained myself with fantasy heroics that pitted me against creatures of enormous girth, extraordinary strength, and fierce cunning. However, this did nothing to free me. As one might guess, a make-believe sword has little effect on genuine problems. I soon grew anxious enough to reach for a real, solid stick in hopes of prying my foot loose.

To my great relief, the stick worked like magic and forced up the pearly rock. To my great astonishment, I discovered that what had snagged my foot was no rock. It had a peculiar shape; the unburied end tapered off to a sharp point. But the fact that it rose in the air of its own accord proved most convincing.

I staggered backwards, succumbing to greater degrees of shock with every inch this mysterious item rose off the ground. I gasped aloud as it was joined by four near-identical ivory hooks. It wasn't until the sharp tips came together that it dawned on me what I was seeing. The pale, pointed rocks were claws! Five claws attached to crusty fingers that formed a fist larger than my pitiful, scrawny mass!

I could feel my face drain of color standing there, wanting to flee, yet powerless to command my muscles to move. White as a ghost, I watched the green, muddy hillside grow taller and taller while taking on a beastly form. I cannot recall if I breathed at all during the time this thrilling phenomenon took place, but the creature extended its neck and breathed a waft of hot air down upon me as if conveying irritation at having had its nap disturbed.

There I stood staring up at two glowing golden eyes, facing a magnificent dragon as real and alive as the hopeful, young knight at its feet. My heart started with fright at what sounded like a boom of thunder, and I fell to the ground like a rag doll. Under a sudden shadow, I realized the dragon's wings had snapped open, mimicking a clap of thunder. The air seemed to swoop up the beast in defiance of gravity, and it took my dragon far, far away while I watched, mouth agape. I stared at the sky until no visible proof remained of what I had witnessed. And though I told many a soul the truth of the matter, none believed me.

I have yet to cross paths again with that golden-eyed dragon, but you will find me still climbing hills where the winds blow hot. With watchful eyes and a solid Terillian sword in my grip, I search for unusual rocks as white and smooth as pearls.

July 17th

When someone tells me to "just relax," I wonder why they don't hand me a book?

July 18th

Hey, pretty book, why don't you lie in my lap awhile?

July 19th

Sipping tea
    with glee
    beneath a gooseberry tree.
I wish Alice were here.
Oh, my dear,
    do not fear,
    she will be.

July 20th

Books are carnival rides for your imagination.

July 21st

To look in the mirror and smile is a challenge for many people. Those who do so without the slightest scowl are indeed fortunate.

July 22nd

The secret to style is a beautiful smile.

July 23rd

Smile.
Steel it.
Keep steeling it.

> *Laugh.*
> Trill it.
> Keep trilling it.

> > *Love.*
> > Feel it.
> > Keep feeling it.

July 24th

The best bubbly I ever tasted was laughter.

July 25th

Laughter can deflate almost any problem down to its proper size.

July 26th

Laugh, and the world longs to be your friend.

July 27th

Quit acting like everything is so serious. Most situations aren't as bad as you fear, and those that are might benefit from a little laughter.

July 28th

Superman's scourge is kryptonite. Fear's kryptonite is laughter.

July 29th

It is in the midst of laughter that our perspective alters and we realize this trying life can still be enjoyed.

July 30th

Ha ha ha ha!
    Tee-hee-hee!
Mwa-ha mwa-ha!
    Kee kee kee!
Ho ho ho ho!
    Haw-hee-haw!
Heh heh heh heh!
    Gah guffaw!
Hoo hoo hoo hoo!
    Hoi hoi-eee!
Ba ha ha ha!
    Tsee tsee tsee!
Giggle, titter,
    snicker, crow,
laughter makes
    my "happy" grow!

July 31st

The elixir of life is a bubbling stream of laughter.

AUGUST

— Ikuchi —
The coiling, sea dragon.

August 1ˢᵗ

If you mess with dragons, you will get burned.
Don't say no one warned you.

August 2ⁿᵈ

"While fun is desirable, regret is quite the
opposite."

—from ***Eena, The Curse of Wanyaka Cave***

August 3ʳᵈ

Many of us draw lines which we intend never to
cross.
But life tests our resolve, mercilessly at times,
and a foot budges, nudged past that thinly-drawn
line. So we draw another, resolving never to
cross this one. Days grow dark and fog creeps in
to blind our view, clouding the reason for the

line's existence from our minds. We draw another mark, ashamed that the last was crossed with less coaxing than we imagined it would require. Shadows and doubts give further need to draw a new line, and then another and another. Lines, I think, are too slim and obscure to be dependable deterrents for behavior. Too often, too easily, people stumble into places they later regret entering. What, then, keeps some individuals from crossing those narrow lines?

It is the power of values.

For if a person possessing values were to step one foot outside their line, they would be forced to release hands with those inflexible values and consciously abandon them. But their values are persuasive, keeping a tight grip, warding off the luring temptations beckoning one to test the line. Thus values maintained keep a person safely away from areas they dare not travel, steering a life between the lines, enhancing willpower and shaping mighty strength of character.

August 4th

Some days I feel like my worth is being reevaluated every five minutes.

August 5th

The real me isn't someone you see but someone you know.

August 6th

The day you were born
Heaven wept at its great loss,
Earth joyed at its gain.

August 7th

I once dreamt that the man in the moon took an interest in me and reflected the sun's light directly in my path, lighting the way for my footsteps to sink themselves into the ground. It was wonderful to have my course illuminated by one with a grander perspective than my own. But when I awoke, realizing I could not call on the moon for guidance, my spirit sank until it occurred to me I could talk to the one who had created the moon. And He has lit my path ever since.

August 8th

If every day you were to walk past the same
individual and ignore him, never smiling or
saying hello or returning any kind gesture he
extended toward you, would you expect that
same individual to readily respond if suddenly
you were to implore his helping hand? Then
don't ignore God. Say 'hello' now and then.

August 9th

If you dream your problems at night and live
your problems by day, you are suffering the
effects of paralyzing toxins delivered by the sting
of worry, stress, and fear. You must detach
yourself from these leeches if you do not wish to
be irreversibly poisoned.

August 10th

Life can seem like a gloomy wait in the thick of
black shadows.
And still there are those who smile at the
darkness, anticipating the beauty of an eventual
sunrise.

August 11th

Personal problems appear big because we press
our nose to the glass to observe them. This only
serves to magnify our troubles. The problems of
others we tend to view at a reasonable distance,
making their woes and bothers appear ordinary.
Too bad we don't naturally take a few steps back
before considering our own plight.

August 12th

There is a sky full of stars aplenty, and all you
can babble about is a cold, little rock we call the
moon. This is how it is with petty problems that
exist too close to us.

August 13th

You won't solve your problems by drowning
others in them.

August 14th

I felt sad.
I felt cold.
I felt hurt.
I felt forsaken and lonely.
105

I felt doubtful and hesitant.
I felt scared and deeply worried.
I felt different, unknown, and unwelcome.
I felt empty and woefully neglected.
I felt weak and intimidated.
I felt withdrawn and shy.
I felt utterly hopeless.
Then you held my hand,
and I felt better.

August 15th

While *"Once upon a time"* may be a great way
to start a story, *"Here in the moment"* is the best
way to live one.

August 16th

I sometimes wonder if life isn't a giant mirror
that reflects back at me everything I hold up to it.

August 17th

Not every day is awful.
Not every day is good.
Despite the way the hours pass
I'm living like I should.

Not every day is all wrong.
Not every day is right.
At least I'm not a spider
trying to scamper out of sight.

Not every day is ideal.
Not every day is bad.
At any rate I have my senses
even if they're mad.

Not every day is happy.
Not every day is glum.
When sadness drags me in the dumps
A simple tune I hum.

Not every day I smile.
Not every day I frown.
With effort, I can take a scowl
and turn it upside down.

Not every day is crazy.
Not every day is sane.
If consequence nips at my heels
I don't pass on the blame.

Not every day is giddy.
Not every day is blah.
Yet I can still appreciate
a giggle and guffaw.

Not every day is timid.
Not every day is proud.
I may not be a dragon
but I roar about as loud.

Not every day has rainbows.
Not every day has rain.
Despite the fact I'm stiff and sore,
I'm not in chronic pain.

On every day the sun shines,
so every night I pray
that I might see the morning light
and live another day.

August 18th

A sunrise is a wondrous marvel, but in reality the
sun never rises. It is the earth that rotates to face
the sun. Life too can be a wondrous marvel, but
like the earth, we must turn our eyes toward
brighter things.

August 19th

You are right, I do fall down a lot.
But that wouldn't be true if I never stood back
up.

August 20th

Life is not about having perfect days. Life is not about handling days perfectly. Life is about perfecting one's character through the having and handling of every given day.

August 21st

No one can convince a man of his erring ways as persuasively as experience.

August 22nd

Should-haves are the devil's greatest tool against our personal progress. He shouts in our ears that they are failures, while God calmly whispers they are lessons.

August 23rd

Had life not given me reasons to grieve, I would never have known the healing power of a hug.

August 24th

Pain defines moments in the lives of all human beings. The trial is not the endurance of pain but the choices we make regarding how to endure.

August 25th

Life is a test. Without problems to solve, it wouldn't be much of a test.

August 26th

Curiosity killed the cat, but not before teaching her that honey bees are not sweet, tweeting birds are slow to react, mice can serve as both toys and food, big dogs like to snuggle, falling isn't flying, cream drips from lazy cows, water should be avoided at all costs, baths don't require getting wet, kindness and cruelty often fall from the same hand, and engines remain comfortably warm long after the motor dies.

August 27th

Life's lessons aren't always new. Often they're the same old worn-out truths offering us greater depths of wisdom and understanding.

August 28th

Mistakes focus our minds on specific details. They weed out truths and afford us goals, bringing straight to our attention lessons to be learned. Mistakes are not meant to make us failures; they are meant to make us wise.

August 29th

If all of our sins, bad habits, and poor choices were permanently inked into our skin like tattoos, we would all dress quite modestly.

August 30th

Life's greatest lessons were not shown to me, read to me, illustrated or explained to me; they happened to me.

August 31st

Some things can't be taught; they can only be discovered.

SEPTEMBER

— Zmey —
The dragon that leaves fiery wakes.

September 1st

Behind my house within walking distance is a big, beautiful hill. I fell in love with it growing up as a child years ago. I would look to the hill many times a day, studying its mossy spots; its hairy, golden veins; and the muddy flecks that mimicked a scattering of bulbous rocks. Because of the hill, I learned to adore the evening sunset for unusual reasons no one would ever believe. Not because the red sun dyed the hump of my hill a dark maroon when the two appeared to touch. And not because of the way the sky mixed rosy and smoky clouds together as they reached down from above…or up from below— it was hard to say which way they swirled. No, the reason I loved the sunset enough to watch it faithfully every night, either from up on the rooftop or from a private spot in the cattails near the creek below my house, was because that beautiful hill showed me twice in a night the same marvelous sunset.

First upside up. And then upside down.

Please don't laugh. The sun did indeed set twice in a night for me. My mother would laugh whenever I tried to convince her it was true. More than once I persuaded her to sit and watch, directing her eyes to a small rise attached to the steeper hill next to it. When the final red tinge of sun vanished completely and the world went dark, I would look to the lesser rise, knowing a red sun would manifest itself once again on its rugged face.

"Look, Mama, look! You will see it! The sun will show itself again, it will! And it will set upside down—I'm not lying!"

But no matter how long she waited, her patience was never long enough. "Silly girl," she would say. "I see nothing but stars."

"But it's true, Mama! The sun will show itself again if you wait."

And she did wait.

But it didn't show in all that time.

"It must be an illusion," she finally decided, believing her daughter would not lie. "Perhaps the moon reflects the sun onto that rise on rare nights."

"On every night, Mama," I corrected.

Her smile was playful and doubtful at the same time. She then walked away sighing, "Oh, silly girl."

Alone I would wait until, as faithfully as ever, the red sun appeared on the smaller rise, divided by a vertical wisp of black. Slowly, surely, it sank upside down until it disappeared.

And so it was I grew to be a young woman in love with a magical hill—for that is the logical conclusion I drew at its repeating of an upturned sunset each night for my eyes only. Mother, though she never witnessed the miracle, labeled it an illusion. I dubbed it magic. For what else could explain a single sun setting twice within a span of minutes, and topsy-turvy at that? I will admit there were occasions when I stood on my head in the grass, feet propped high against the trunk of an oak tree, in order to see the second sunset properly. Never with Mother nearby. For she would surely gasp and say, "How terribly unladylike!"

One cloudy evening, only a few sunsets after my seventeenth birthday, I was nearing my quiet spot amongst the cattails by the creek when something stirred in my stomach. It felt awful. At the same time, I glimpsed a figure move within the cattails, but I had no idea if what I'd find there would prove as awful as my stomach's uneasiness seemed to anticipate. For those who doubt, I emphatically insist that it is a wise rule to listen to your stomach. It has an uncanny sense about the reality of things. On this

115

particular occasion I failed to heed that uncomfortable warning and continued cautiously forward to my spot within the cluster of tall cattails. My stomach did a somersault when a very large man stepped out into the open and faced me. He was smiling in a manner that could never—even by the most naïve minds—be mistaken for friendly.

I turned to run back to the house, but I was grabbed by the man who lunged at me with the speed of a cobra. He yanked my body to him. When my lungs filled with air, preparing to scream, he stifled the sound with a firm hand, smothering my face. Desperate to breath, I tried in vain to pry his fingers away. He dragged me into the cattails before slipping his hand down off my nose, allowing me to draw in oxygen but still barring any ability to scream. As the man growled in my ear, insensible words dripping with malice, I feared for my life.

"They thought they could hide you from me, that I wouldn't detect your putrid stench out here in the middle of nowhere. But I swore to them I'd hunt you down—every last one of you. So far I've kept my word. I've diminished your numbers and robbed you of those abominable service creatures. And I never stopped searching for you, young one—in caves and deserts and every other inhospitable corner of existence. I

116

even bribed the vagrant sailors of pirate ships, thinking they might find you in transport when your superiors finally decided to call you overseas. But no—you're not quite old enough to be summoned yet. So I'll kill you now as I did the others. I'll end your life before it becomes my misfortune. When you're dead, I'll wait here for your service creatures to show their vile forms, and then I will slay them as well."

I was sucking in air through my nose while these words hit my ear, void of meaning. Nothing he said made the least amount of sense to me. Surely, he had mistaken me for a hostile individual capable of causing him torment.

I was no one to fear. No one at all.

His fingers clamped down over my nose once again as if he meant to suffocate the life out of me. I fought him with all my might, knowing my struggles were futile; his strength far surpassed my own. My eyes flickered back at the hill I loved so much as if to say "goodbye," at which time I caught a peculiar sight. Two suns were visible at once—one red orb hanging above the hill and a second orb aglow on the face of the lower rise. I thought, perhaps, that my senses were being impaired by lack of oxygen.

When the ground quaked beneath my feet, it seemed as if the planet itself had chosen to come to my rescue. The tremors managed to pull the grassy footing from beneath my assailant. He tumbled over and his hands flailed outward, releasing me. Coughing and gasping for air, I scrambled to get away from him, deterred by the shaking ground until it suddenly ceased. My eyes darted from the grass to my beloved hill, only to find that it was gone! The setting sun hung low in the sky over a completely flat horizon!

I was about to flee for home, more concerned for self-preservation than the miraculous disappearance of an entire hill, when the man shrieked, making my eyes turn back to him. My body slowly followed suit, astounded by what registered in my sight.

My would-be killer was on the ground looking up into the face of an ominous, hovering beast kept aloft by giant wings. The body of the creature was humped, covered in mossy spots and hairy, golden veins and muddy, bulbous flecks that resembled exactly the missing hill. It dawned on me that the low rise normally sitting adjacent to the hill was the beast's head. I knew this without a doubt because a red eye glared from the side of its head, mimicking the sun at dusk. I gasped, realizing my beloved hill was in actuality a dragon! My topsy-turvy sunset wasn't at all a second sunset but a dragon's bright eye which opened up each and every

118

evening to look out at the world before vanishing under dragon eyelids.

I wondered, was this beast a service creature like those the vile man had muttered about in my ear? There would be no asking him, for he was swallowed whole by the beast in question, scarcely able to let out a final shriek.

The dragon's face turned to stare at me full on, revealing two glowing, red eyes. My stomach felt calm, but in my mind I feared this was no service creature but a monster that meant to feed on me as it had the unfortunate man. The dragon made no sudden moves, however, and the dagger-like teeth I had glimpsed in its mouth were not shown to me again. The dragon lowered its head. Cautiously I approached, moving just close enough to reach out and touch its snout. As my fingers made contact with the scaly texture of its skin, a waft of swirly, gray smoke puffed from both nostrils, startling me, convincing my feet to scuttle backwards. Its immense body rotated in the air, and I watched in awe as a pair of giant wings took the creature back to its resting place where once again he appeared as a distant hill blocking out the setting sun.

"Thank you," I breathed as the dragon closed its eyes.

I immediately ran to the house to relay the entire story to my mother who became greatly agitated at my mention of a stranger, and then greatly perturbed at my insistence that a man-eating dragon did indeed live past the creek behind our house. The truth was ultimately labeled an outlandish illusion, and I was informed by my mother that a career in story-telling might very well suit me.

That was all about a year ago today. And I shall never forget the life-changing moment I discovered that the hill I loved was in truth a dragon I loved even more. Now, as I turn eighteen, my stomach twists itself up into knots. I have learned to listen to it, for its predictions have yet to be wrong. I know something is coming. A change in my life and in the world itself. What sort of change, I don't know. But I am sure it involves me and my dragon. The great beast has awakened for the second time in my young life, but I have no fear. It intends to take me somewhere. Somewhere I am needed. And when my mother sees that I and the great hill behind our house are both gone, she might come to believe in my illusions.....and in dragons.

September 2nd

You cannot know what I do not tell you, yet you will be judged harshly for not knowing.

September 3rd

No one believes he is an idiot until the consequences of his actions prove it. Then hindsight rubs it in.

September 4th

Why is the eye considered a reliable judge when it knows nothing of love or intelligence?

September 5th

Knowledge gained is as useless as pride
If filed away and never applied.

September 6th

"Books are full of useful knowledge," my professor would say at the end of nearly every lecture.

One bright spring day he took our class outdoors to show us a prickly cactus that was both very wide and very tall. It wasn't an uncommon sight around campus. At the top of the cactus a balloon seemed to hover about a foot above. It would have floated away if not for a string tied to it, the opposite end caught in the needles of the cactus plant. It was impossible for anyone to reach the balloon for the height of the plant and the long, threatening spikes protruding from every inch of its skin. The professor explained that we were to come up with a way to retrieve the balloon without popping it and without harming the cactus or ourselves.

"Books are full of useful knowledge," he repeated for the umpteenth time as he untarped a pickup full of hardbound books. We were allowed a brief time to browse through them and the wide variety of topics they included before he began to ask individual students which books they would choose to use to solve the problem of the balloon and the cactus.

"I would use the books on robotics," one person responded. "A long robotic arm could reach the balloon and safely retrieve it."

"I think the books about ropes and knots might work," replied another student, "I could try lassoing the balloon."

"Maybe a few books on cactus care would be useful," said someone else. "It might include instructions on safely removing needles from the plant without harming it. Then I could climb up the bare area of the cactus and grab the balloon."

"Books on aviation could teach me how to fly a helicopter up there," someone said, eliciting a few snickers. Impractical but creative.

"Or just make a small, remote-control flying machine," came a wise retort.

"I know, I know," piped up an equally creative student, "A couple books on NASA space suits and trampolines and I could bounce high enough to snatch up the balloon in protective gear." After a moment of laughter, the professor asked one girl who normally kept quiet unless called upon.

"Which books would you suggest using to solve the problem?" Without hesitating, she gave a ready answer.

"All of them."

The professor perked a curious eyebrow and repeated her response. "All of them?"

"Yes," the girl nodded. "I would pile them against the cactus in a set of steps and climb up and remove the balloon."

Indeed, there is useful book knowledge, but even more useful is never abandoning your flat out good sense.

September 7th

To get it done
and see it thru,
        find less to say
        and more to do.

September 8th

None of us have reached the peak of perfection,
but it shouldn't stop anyone from trying to make
the climb.

September 9th

Life has me trapped in a cocoon of earth where I
must grow and change until the day I sprout
wings. And on that day I shall burst free, no
longer marooned on a pebble of dust in a
universe that only waits for me to find a means to
fly.

September 10th

To actively improve the world
and change your life as well,
speak all the good you know,
and all the bad refuse to tell.

124

September 11th

I might be tempted to socialize more if the conversations taking place around me were half as interesting as the dialogue going on inside my head.

September 12th

Have you ever noticed how the most intriguing individual in the room seems content to listen sooner than speak?

September 13th

The ears and the heart are connected, it's true, for when ears open wide, the heart opens up too.

September 14th

I do listen. I just wait for the words to stop and your eyes to speak.

September 15th

Anyone who takes the time to attentively listen is either an old soul or a romantic one.

September 16th

Birthdays were made for going wild over the people we think are amazing.

September 17th

Eyes speak louder than words; life is precious; hate is poison; God is the best of all possible friends; silence and time are valuable treasures; happiness can be just as powerful in pretend; and soft licorice is a temptation in any color, especially exotic black.

September 18th

Happiness is a frame of mind. It is a state of thinking. It is an attitude, a headset, a mentality. Happiness is a disposition and demeanor. It is a mood and sensibility. It is a philosophy, a notion, a tone, an outlook and perspective. Happiness is all of these things, none of which exist separate from me. They cannot be extracted or stolen because they constitute my very being. Therefore, happiness must be the natural essence of me.

September 19th

The secret to happiness is elusive because it is a paradoxical truth. To gain happiness, you must first cease pursuing it. Things perceived to provide happiness are like shiny, pretty bubbles that lure us this way and that way, chasing after their glossy buoyancy. But once they are handled, they pop—empty—vanishing along with the hope that happiness could ever be captured. Happiness cannot be caught or won or purchased or even handled. It simply forms like a rainbow in the kindest and most grateful hearts.

September 20th

It is not wrong to feel sorry for yourself. Just like it is not wrong to sit in a puddle of water while the rain pours down on your head. But neither is productive, unless you enjoy feeling cold and miserable and soggy while mascara runs down your face.

September 21st

It is a fight to let go of a past that refuses to withdraw its sticky tentacles from your present.

September 22nd

Life isn't always kind. It isn't gentle and loving or sympathetic to the pains and sorrows of humanity. I, however, as an individual in control of my own actions, can be kind and loving, gentle and sympathetic to those around me, and in the process improve what life is for everyone.

September 23rd

Out of all the magic words in existence, kind words produce the most powerful transformation spells.

September 24th

I am not what you see.
I am what time and effort and interaction slowly unveil.

September 25th

Art doesn't bare itself to just anyone, but to believers called artists.

September 26th

Art and the artist meet in stages, slowly revealing themselves until both are satisfied with what the other has become.

September 27th

An artist is merely a tool with which art molds itself.

September 28th

The moon is my fear.
The sun is my heart afire.
The stars, my love songs.

September 29th

The crazy thing about poetry is how its simplicity makes it complicated.

September 30th

A poet is simply an artist whose medium is human emotions. A poet chisels away at our own sensibilities, shaping our vision while molding our hearts. A poet wraps words around our own feelings and presents them as fresh gifts to humanity.

OCTOBER

The second dragon, fierce and attacking.

October 1st

A dragon grows in leaps and bounds,
Like troubles mounting by the pound.

Its stature heightens day to day,
Imposing dread and deep dismay.

A paralyzing roar it gains
While from its snout hot fire rains.

It sees you shrink. Your fear it knows.
And by the hour the nightmare grows.

Unless you slay the dragon soon,
Your troubles may become your doom.

October 2nd

Dragons are a manifestation of things we fear.
More often than not, those fears prove to be just
as daunting and just as imaginary.

131

October 3rd

Fearing the night won't keep the sun from setting.

October 4th

Fear comes at me like a massive bull with lowered horns ready to gore. But I have learned of the insubstantial nature of fear: if I stand my ground, it will pass right through me.

October 5th

Fear is not respect. It is but a conniving, little weasel next to that mighty lion. They are a far, far cry from the same animal.

October 6th

If we were to behave half as well as we believe others ought to behave, we might prove ourselves as grand in character as excuses and justifications prevent us from being.

October 7th

I'm sorry. Oh, what simple words are these!
I'm sorry. Lips should breathe them out with
ease!
But nay, in barring up the way,
"I'll die first" are the words you say.
I'm sorry, woe is all pride guarantees.

October 8th

Pride is not your friend.
He would have you think he is, that he affords
you strength and courage, but in truth he robs
you of your health and by slow, diluted degrees
steals your might. He is a crafty and cunning liar
who would have you think that stubborn,
unapologetic, superior, boastful, and popular are
admirable traits. Pride would convince you that
being right is more crucial than being kind. He
would have you sever relationships, even turn
your back on family and friends rather than utter
a humble apology. To do so is beneath you,
pride would say. He would have you fight like a
raptor and gnash your teeth while jutting out an
inflexible jaw to defend and protect him,
regardless of who is hurt in the process. He
would use and demean you in order to puff up

and fortify himself. He would destroy your life and every meaningful association before casting you aside without a hint of remorse.

Again, Pride is not your friend.

October 9th

Just say "I'm sorry." It's not a tongue twister. It does not need repeating multiple times. The phrase is simple and short, easy to articulate. And the last time I checked, it sounded just as good—if not better—in a whisper. So just say it; say "I'm sorry."

October 10th

The hero isn't the one who is right, but the one who steps forward to take the blame—deserved or not—and apologize to save a relationship.

October 11th

We live our lives supposing things are as they appear to be when that is almost never the case.

October 12th

Afraid of offending with an off word or the slightest insensitivity, I keep an unobtrusive and silent distance. Nevertheless, my pursed lips and offish stance are perceived as cold, managing to offend all.

October 13th

Vultures pick the meat clean off a bone. Guilt eats at the marrow, leaving a man hollow.

October 14th

I can overlook the lie; what's harder to ignore is the grotesque way it has marred your character.

October 15th

A pang of guilt, like a blaring siren, should never be ignored.

October 16th

Guilt cannot change you; it can only hint that there's something worth your effort to change.

October 17th

This feeling of guilt is your conscience calling your attention to the higher road, and your heart wishing you had taken it.

October 18th

Consider guilt like a street sign that warns of rough roads ahead if you don't make a u-turn.

October 19th

When dragons attack, the only thing you should seek to stand behind is your own sword.

October 20th

It was never my intent to get lost in the woods, for I truly believed if I followed the river in, I could certainly retrace my steps and follow it out to the very point where I had ducked through the trees. The theory seemed quite logical at the time, and yet looking back, I see how silly it is to think that logical is synonymous with correct.

I had seen a bird. That's where this story begins. It was a remarkable bird. Indeed, it

136

would have to have been remarkable to have lured me into the woods despite the frightful way my mother always verbally painted the dark mysteriousness of the forest. But a tempting sort of curiosity gripped me when that spectacularly-colorful bird swooped down from the air, low enough to enter the trees. I estimated its size as comparable to an eagle. It was brightly-painted enough to have been some variety of parrot, yet I swore by the looks of its outspread wings that this flying creature had lost all of its feathers. Either that, or it had been born without a single one. During the brief few moments I observed the thing, it seemed more like a neon penguin with a glider attached to its back than an actual naturally-feathered bird, but I knew that such a curiosity could not be so. Hence, you see my dilemma—why, despite ample and adamant parental warnings, I simply had to step into the woods and discover what this wonderful, flying peculiarity was.

I managed to follow glimpses of bright reds and yellows weaving through the trees, which quickly led me to a river. It was not a loud, scary, fast-flowing river like one in which a person might fear drowning. It was rather a quiet, shallow, meandering water as clear as glass in its appearance—glass that flows and ripples, which glass does not do, but this river was just as clear, allowing a smooth bed of gray and blue rocks to be easily seen as if I were looking at them through a long, glass window.

At any rate, I lost sight of the featherless bird after running beside the riverbank for a short way. When I turned back around to try and spot the trees through which I had entered the forest, I could not see them. I began to think that perhaps in my haste I had actually come a longer way than I had first assumed. It crossed my mind that a little deeper trek into the forest at this point could hardly make a longer way any longer, so I dared to follow the river, believing, as I said before, that what guided me in would also guide me out.

Nothing seemed out of the ordinary at all, and I would have had no idea that things were in fact extraordinary had I not stopped to stand on a rock for a bit too long. While shading my eyes in order to get a better glimpse of any bright colors somewhere among the trees, I stood on that rock when it unexpectedly began to wiggle and tremble, forcing me to concentrate on keeping my balance. I did so quite impressively until the rock opened its mouth and spoke.

"Get off me!" it said. "Get off me, you big-footed bendy!"

Astonished and slightly offended, I stepped aside onto another rock, not at all expecting it to complain as well.

"You're heavier than you think! Get off me, you brutish bendy!"

Equally as astonished, for I could not be any moreso, I stepped aside again, careful this time not to set foot on any sort of pebble or stone or object that resembled the other rocks. I am quite certain that my eyes grew as wide as saucers, as they say, when the rocks upon which I had been standing rose up entirely from the ground to their full height, which turned out to be just below my kneecap. It was only the two. They were both short, gray characters with stubby extensions for arms and legs, though lacking a toe on each foot and a finger on each hand. Their heads seemed blended as one with their torsos, and I had to look very hard to see a pair of gray lips and gray eyes which lacked any coloring. It didn't appear that either had a nose; however, it was easy enough to imagine the jagged area between mouth and eyes as a sort of bumpy-nose appendage.

"Begging your pardon," I said, "but I am not at all a brutish bendy."

The dwarfish rocks eyed me skeptically. "Then what do you call it when you stand on someone's head who doesn't want you to be standing on their head?"

"Brutish!" his companion blurted out before my tongue could begin to form a reply.

"But I didn't know I was standing on anyone's head," I declared in my defense. "Had I known that common rocks were actually very uncommon heads, I would never have placed my feet upon them."

"That's what they all say," the pair grumbled in unison. I, of course, instantly wondered how many others had stumbled across these two talking rocks.

"And it's the last thing they ever say," an entirely new voice informed me. There was no mistaking the caustic threat in his words.

I glanced around, scanning over the tops of a few hundred other rocks along the riverbank, hoping to spot this new, unfriendly speaker. At a peripheral streak of movement, my eyes darted sidelong and upward to catch the moving limbs of a tree. I watched in awe as facial features magically developed on a higher portion of the trunk. As soon as I realized that the tree was reaching for me—its twiggy fingers intending to wrap themselves around me—I ducked and jumped out of the way.

Swiveling on my feet, I rushed back up the riverbank toward home....or so I thought. Luck seemed to be with me as I managed to escape the tree that threatened my life, but then I found my flight halted when tens of hundreds of seemingly-ordinary rocks popped out of the ground on four-toed feet, ready to bar my way. It was a frightening scene, these rock creatures climbing on each other's heads, which apparently wasn't as disagreeable an occurrence as the first two had led me to believe. They began to pen me in, forming a tighter and tighter circle while climbing upon each other, creating an enclosed rock wall. Meanwhile, a low and disturbing chant started up among them.

"Crush the bendy! Crush the bendy! Crush the bendy!"

Desperate and frightened, I resolved to knock over the creatures and make an attempt at plowing my way through to freedom when an unfamiliar voice called out above the others. Its volume and assertiveness effectively stopped every one of us in our aims. The awful chanting ceased at once.

"Leave the bendy alone!" the voice commanded. "Can't you see she's an unusually?"

A collective gasp echoed all around me, and I observed how the rock aggressors leaned warily away from me as if I were the carrier of a deadly boulder disease. I couldn't help but ask aloud,

"I'm unusually what?" I glanced about, searching for the one who had saved me from being crushed by these animated rocks.

"Not what, but *who*," the voice said. "It's who you are that's frightening; you're one of...*them*."

"One of them?" I still couldn't identify to whom I was speaking, but his voice fell low and mysterious as he breathed a reply.

"One of the unusuallies."

I had to crinkle my brow. "I don't believe that's a real word."

"I don't believe *you're* a real word."

My brow crinkled up tighter. "That makes no sense at all."

I huffed a sound of irritation, noticing at this point that the wall made of dwarfish rocks was beginning to part from the very back, creating a separation that was making its way toward me. I kept my eyes on it, anxious to see what or who would emerge from the opening.

"You make no sense at all," the voice groused, "which is why I know you are an unusually."

"Oh for Pete's sake," I exclaimed with exasperation, "I'm unusually what?"

A tiny man stepped out from where the wall of rocks parted. At first I thought him to be some sort of gnome, until I realized that underneath his red floppy hat, yellow raincoat, oval glasses missing both lenses, and a fuzzy beard that closely resembled white moss—underneath all of it existed another gray rock creature. The quality of his voice, as well as his useless glasses, made him seem much older and wiser than the others— if one can effectively judge such a thing in that manner. He ignored my question and turned to glare at the others, pointing the tip of his cane from figure to figure as he proceeded to awe the crowd with a speech.

"Beware, my dears. You know we are defenseless against the formidable unusuallies. But this one here; she is a young one, not old enough to be a real threat to us yet. Therefore, I must take her away and learn of her magic so we can defend ourselves against the others if ever they show their faces here again."

A chorus of mystified oohs and aahhs rose from the surrounding rock dwarfs.

"Now, be off with you before she casts a sleeping spell upon your heads!"

As fast as they had gathered, the tens of hundreds of rocks scrambled back to the riverbank and disappeared—all but the top of their hard crowns—into the sand. I was left alone with my gnomish rescuer. He scrutinized me with what seemed like a disapproving scowl and then waved his cane downstream before

143

taking a step himself in that direction. I was certain the gesture meant for me to follow.

We walked in silence for a period of time. Though I glanced around looking for evidence of other rock creatures or featherless birds or trees with twiggy fingers, I saw none. Eventually, I dared to speak.

"Who are you? What is this strange place?"

The little man made a grunting sound and batted a hand behind him, letting me know he would not be answering my questions.

"I'm not magic, you know," I told him.

I could see humor in his eye and a smirk beneath his mossy beard as he peered over his shoulder at me. "You don't say," he chuckled. Apparently the news came as no surprise to him.

We veered away from the river and weaved our way through a thick area of trees.

"Why did you call me an unusually?" I asked. I was surprised when he actually responded.

"Because you are not usual."

"Oh." As opposed to everyday talking rocks, I thought to myself.

The little man stopped in his tracks. His cane rose from the ground and pointed straight ahead between a tight row of trees and leafy shrubbery. "Head on through there."

I questioned him with a look, but he continued to point with his cane, staring ahead at where he wanted me to go. I took a tentative, obedient step but then hesitated, wondering where the path would lead and why he wanted me to step through first. When I glanced back, the rock-gnome was gone. Mustering up a bit of courage by convincing myself that it would be foolishness to save a person only to send her into danger, I pushed through the line of trees and shrubbery. To my great astonishment, I found myself standing in my own backyard, precisely where I had first followed the bright, featherless bird into the woods.

How very unusual, I thought, to travel so far along the river and then end up in the exact same place I started. But then again—I smiled to myself, feeling a newfound sense of pride—I am, after all, an unusually.

October 21ˢᵗ

"Silly little monster" all would say.
They'd scratch its head and turn away
until it snatched their tiny noses.
They couldn't even smell the roses!
Ever after, every child
dreaded monsters, fierce or mild.

145

October 22nd

Fear confronted me, and I stood paralyzed. He
seemed a formidable, abiding presence.
Then a voice whispered, "Fear not."
Fear not, I thought with desperate longing. Oh,
how I wanted to heed those words—but how?
Hour after hour, day after day, fear refused to
budge while I remained paralyzed. And so I let
him make my choices; what else could I do?
Alas, he never once chose well for me.

October 23rd

Fear never scaled one mountain, never stepped
up on a stage, never accepted a challenge, never
tilled new ground, never walked in a race; he
never even dared to dream. Fear failed to slay a
single dragon. Remember that before you choose
to keep his company.

October 24th

A pumpkin lives but once a year
when someone sets its soul afire
and on that night it stirs up fear
until its flame is snuffed.
But e'en one night of eerie light is fright enough.

October 25th

The jack-o-lantern follows me with tapered,
glowing eyes.
His yellow teeth grin evily. His cackle I despise.
But I shall have the final laugh when Halloween
is through.
This pumpkin king I'll split in half to make a pie
for two.

October 26th

A Halloween flower,
if ever there was one,
would smell like an onion,
have thorns like a rose.

With charcoal black petals
and vines that entangle,
t'would grow under moonlight
in mud, I suppose.

October 27th

The whispers you hear in your ear that you fear
in the air everywhere,
they are ghosts.

The moans and the groans in the lowest of tones
no one owns or condones,
they are ghosts.

You might deem them gremlins or water or wind,
while others say shadows or rodents or sin.

But oh! I say no!
'Tis not so, child, for lo!
The chills that you feel in a thrill that proves
goose
bumps are frightfully real,
they are ghosts!

October 28th

Witches cackle.
Goblins growl.
Specters boo,
And werewolves howl.
Black cats hiss.
Bats flap their wings.
Mummies moan.
The cold wind sings.
Ogre's roar.
And crows, they caw.
Vampires bahahahaha.
Warlocks swish their moonlit capes.

Loch Ness monsters churn the lake.
Skeletons, they rattle bones
While graveyards crack the old headstones.
All the while the ghouls, they cry
To trick-or-treaters passing by.
Oh, the noise on Halloween;
It makes me want to scream!

October 29th

Treats and tricks.
Witch broomsticks.
Jack-o-lanterns
Lick their lips.

Crows and cats.
Vampire bats.
Capes and fangs
And pointed hats.

Werewolves howl.
Phantoms prowl.
Halloween's
Upon us now.

October 30th

The coldest day in fall
is at the Hallows Evening ball
where ghoulish fun
avoids the sun
as monsters mingle wall to wall.

October 31st

Go put on your mask.
Say "trick-or-treat" in costume.
It's All Hallows Eve.

NOVEMBER

— Imugi —
The young proto-dragon that brings good luck.

November 1ˢᵗ

Isn't it strange how a lamb can feel like a lion when comparing itself to a mouse, whereas a lion feels like a lamb when measuring itself against dragons?

November 2ⁿᵈ

Lift up your eyes and see the good in the world, for we are people with an amazing capacity to do great good. And if only the minority choose to exercise this capacity to the smallest degree, oh how wondrous and sweet the deeds performed at but a few hands!

November 3ʳᵈ

What kind of person is void of compassion? A heartless one. But alas, compassion cannot exist without the endurance of afflictions.

151

November 4ᵗʰ

There's always another option.
There's always another one.
It's never only "this" or "that,"
The moon or else the sun.

Don't sigh and choose the greater
Or lesser of two plights.
But look to see the stars beyond
For options vast and bright.

November 5ᵗʰ

It's easy to be kind to friends who return your smiles and who happily lend a helping hand. But the true test of good character is finding the will and desire to be kind and charitable to those who give us absolutely no motivation to do so.

November 6ᵗʰ

I don't know how to save the world, though I do know it involves a great deal of love and kindness.

November 7th

As a child, I once suffered a bad fall that resulted in scratched palms and scraped knees. I remember how badly it stung, the cold air hitting my bleeding wounds; I felt that I couldn't stand up for the pain. Through a veil of tears, I recall a kind hand reaching for me and helping me to my feet. My knees and palms were washed clean, and I remember thinking that for the rest of my life, I wanted to help people stand back up.

November 8th

If we simply imagined that everyone who crossed our path was living out his or her very last day on Earth, we might treat people as kindly as we ought to each day they lived.

November 9th

You would think those who have endured unkindness would be kinder as a result, intent on sparing others the awful suffering they abhorred firsthand.

November 10ᵗʰ

All human beings wield influence—a powerful sword granted at birth. Wield your sword with care.

November 11ᵗʰ

You can teach a person all you know, but only experience will convince him that what you say is true.

November 12ᵗʰ

Some people do not like you; that's a given. So what?

November 13ᵗʰ

For every one person who praises you, there are a hundred who would criticize. Heed neither the one nor the hundred. It is your own opinion that truly matters.

November 14th

The cup is both half full *and* half empty; it has never been one or the other. Stop obsessing over a trivial point and be thankful you have something to drink.

November 15th

The world seems to want us to be sad and angry because bad things frequently happen. But I say we should feel the opposite. We should be happy and cheerful because good things happen. We should be delighted to see the sun rise and stars glow and rainbows color stormy skies. We should savor every simple breath and eat each meal with gratitude. We should slumber in sweet dreams and relish moments of laughter and love. We should take more notice of the joys and kindnesses that do exist, still dictating the actions of millions of good people all over the world. Life is filled with pleasant moments, not just grief. We should be happy because this is true.

November 16th

Thank you for the day and night,
    for rainy spells and summer's light.

Thank you for the skies of blue
    and puffy clouds in grayish hue.
Thank you for the gigglefests
    and midnight's cloak to hasten rest.
Thank you for tomorrow new
    and yesterday's tomorrow too.
Thank you for "I'm glad we met"
    and also for "we haven't yet."
Thank you for the peace of mind
    a grateful soul doth always find.

November 17th

It is easy to say I am thankful for the sweet and beautiful things in life: flower gardens, ice cream cones, diamond rings, dances under moonlight, children's laughter, birdsongs, and the like. The challenge is recognizing things of value in the dark, sour, uglier parts of life. But if you look hard enough, you will find that even tough times offer pearls worthy of gratitude.

November 18th

Gratitude is a grinning attitude.

November 19th

Find much to be grateful for in every day. Doing so will not only enrich your life, it will bless those around you in ways you may never know.

November 20th

"What are you most thankful for?" she asked. My reply came easily. "Being too blessed to have any hope of answering that question."

November 21st

Thanksgiving is not only being aware of the abundance of good in the world but embracing it.

November 22nd

Oh what marvels fill me with thanksgiving! The deep mahogany of a leaf once green. The feathered fronds of tiny icicles coating every twig and branch in a wintry landscape. The feel of goosebumps thawing after endured frozen temperatures. Both hands clamped around a hot mug of herbal tea. The aromatic whiff of mint under my nose. The stir of emotion from a child's cry for mommy. A gift of love detached of strings. Spotted lilies collecting raindrops in a cupped clump of petals. The vibrant mélange of colors on butterfly wings. The milky luster of a single pearl. Rainbows reflecting off iridescence bubbles. Awe-struck silence evoked by any form of beauty.

Avocado flecks in your eyes.

Warm hands on my face.

Sweetness on the tongue.

The harmony of voices.

An answered prayer.

A pink balloon.

A caress.

A smile.

More.

These have become my treasures
by virtue of thanksgiving.

November 23rd

Have the wisdom to perceive all there is to be thankful for, and then be thankful for the wisdom to perceive things so clearly.

November 24th

Gratitude possesses all the energy of a sunbeam. That is how it makes life blossom.

November 25th

When I count my blessings, I find you in every one.

November 26th

Friendship true is a vow of care.
A warm embrace when in despair.
A loving presence waiting there
to lift a heart, its burdens bear.

Friendship true is an earnest prayer.
A tongue of praise for one's welfare.
A smile 'mid laughs as light as air,
and thoughtfulness most kind and rare.

November 27th

To obtain wealth beyond measure, seek to make more friends than money.

November 28th

"What is so rewarding about friendship?" my son asked, curling his upper lip into a sour expression. "Making friends takes too much time and effort, and for what?"

159

I sat on the edge of his bed, understanding how it might seem simpler to go at life solo. "Friendship has its unique rewards," I told him. "They can be very unpredictable. For instance...." I couldn't help but pause to smile crookedly at an old memory that was dear to my heart. Then I shared with my son an unforgettable incident from my younger years.

"True story. When I was about your age, I decided to try out for a school play. Tryouts were to begin right after the last class of the day; however, I had to run home first to grab a couple props I needed for the monologue I planned to perform during tryouts. Silly me, I had left them at the house that morning. Luckily, I only lived across a long expanse of grassy field that separated the school from the nearest neighborhood. Unluckily, it was raining and I didn't have an umbrella.

"Determined to get what I needed, I raced home, grabbed my props, and tore back across the field while my friend waited under the dry protection of the school's wooden eaves. She watched me run in the rain, gesturing for me to go faster while calling out to hurry up or we would be late.

"Well, the rain was pouring by that time which was added reason for me to move fast; I didn't really want to stand on stage in front of dozens of fellow students looking like a wet rat. Don't ask me why I didn't grab an umbrella from home—teenage pride or lack of focus, I'm not sure—but the increasing rain combined with the hollering from my friend as well as my anxious nerves about trying out for the play had me running far too fast in flat shoes that lacked any tread.

"About a yard from the sidewalk where the grass was worn from foot traffic and consequently muddied from the downpour of rain, I slipped and fell on my hind end. Me, my props, and my dignity slid through the mud and lay there, coated. My things were dripping with mud. I was covered in it. I felt my heart plunge, and I wanted to cry. I probably would have, if it hadn't been for the wonderful thing that happened right then. My crazy friend ran over and plopped herself down in the mud beside me. She wiggled in it, making herself as much a mess as I was. Then she took my slimy hand in hers and pulled us both to our feet. We tried out for the play looking like a couple of swine escaped from a pigsty, laughing the whole time. I never did cry, thanks to my friend.

"So yes, my dear son, friendship has its unique rewards—priceless ones."

November 29th

The horses have stopped
their clippity-clop,
but feet are too slow
for where I must go.
So here I shall stay
until light of day
when clippity-clop
gets my team underway.

November 30th

Night helps us appreciate daylight, while lengthy
days make us yearn for a good stretch of night.

DECEMBER

— Zomok —
The flying magician dragon.

December 1st

Learning to breath fire isn't nearly as extraordinary as learning to breath a word of kindness.

December 2nd

So what if you're right?
So what if you're wrong?
In the end you might be surprised to find that God doesn't care so much about whether you were right or wrong but whether, despite it all, you were kind or cruel.

December 3rd

Imagine the greatness this world would know if kindness were as contagious and enduring as the common cold.

December 4th

The greater self-confidence an individual possesses, the less inclined he is to put down others. This says a lot about those who constantly belittle.

December 5th

Hate is loud. Love, however, is so pleasantly felt it has no need to be heard.

December 6th

I can be tolerant of traffic jams and disorganization, faulty technology, miserable weather, and bland foods. People, however, require more than the cold, grudging favor of being tolerated. They require love.

December 7th

Annoyances are strangely not so annoying when the person responsible has endeared himself to you.

December 8ᵗʰ

Some birthdays make you happy.
Some birthdays bring you down.
Some birthdays make you jump for joy
While others paint a frown.

Regardless of your feelings
Or if you're far or near,
The earth was blessed this special day
When Heaven placed you here.

December 9ᵗʰ

Hope is the fuel within all human souls.
Eliminate hope—nothing moves, nothing grows.

December 10ᵗʰ

It's frustrating when our best efforts to help
people fail. But if we could see life through their
weary eyes and experience their trials with the
same frayed emotions, we might understand why.

December 11ᵗʰ

Life's journey doesn't start on the highest
mountain peak where a clear view of the trail

ahead, obstacles and all, is laid out for us to observe before setting foot on the path. No. Life's journey begins on a low road, in a valley, or even down inside a pit where the trail beyond can only be seen in short stretches, and any obstacles come as they are met. This makes life trying, even scary at times. Have faith that God gave you this life, and hence it is worth seeing through to the end of the trail.

December 12th

My shoulders, broad and sculpted thick, were designed for two useful purposes. The one, to carry heavy loads like cedar logs and beams of steel and now and then the careful transfer of an injured friend to a bed of safety. The other purpose I consider superior, and that is to be, in all circumstances and forever, your headrest and cry pillow whereupon you may leave your heaviest burdens.

December 13th

So you want to improve the world? Then do it. To the next person who crosses your path, say something kind, do something generous, perform

a simple act of service. By doing this on a
regular basis, you will indeed improve the world.

December 14th

Beauty may catch the eye, but a jolly laugh will
lasso the heart.

December 15th

The only two words you should ever say to a
mirror are "Hello, Beautiful."

December 16th

Mirror, mirror on the wall,
I have placed you in my hall
Where I wander every day.
Echo beauty, and you'll stay.

December 17th

Glittering tinsel,
lights, glass balls, and candy canes
dangle from pine trees.

167

December 18th

The Christmas spirit is simply an honest spirit of love for all humanity. It is the force that moves us to give what we can, to help as we are able, and to always be of kind comfort.

December 19th

The spirit of Christmas is a sweet, internal peace that testifies of the power of kindness and charity.

December 20th

It seems there's confusion at this time of year regarding the reason for Christmas.
From shopping for presents to spreading good cheer,
the world makes an overly huge fuss.
But Christmas is not for the gifts we exchange.
It's not about sleigh rides or sweet candy canes.
Nay, Christmas is simple. A time to recall
Christ's gift of atonement He gave to us all.

December 21st

My identity is not important—age, gender, or ethnicity. The year and circumstances make little difference either, other than to know it was a cold Christmas night when this miracle occurred in my life. And though the memories are distinctly mine, vivid and unforgettable as if years had never passed since their transpiring, I sincerely hope through this retelling of events you will acquire every thread of understanding I gained in a remarkable moment of truth.

It was cold enough to snow, yet warm enough to melt every flake that touched the ground. I sat outside on my front porch, bundled in the warmest wrap I could find. Inside, the sounds of merriment tickled my ears—a celebration of Christmas among friends and family. I was missing their exchange of homemade gifts, having put no thought or effort into the task. Christmas didn't thrill me like it seemed to for so many others. And as I sat in the darkness staring up at the twinkling aura of a particularly bright star, I wondered for what reason exactly this holiday existed.

I pulled the wrap more snugly around my shoulders while contemplating a string of traditions practiced yearly at this time. What was the big deal about observing silly rituals? Why the extra jollity and efforts this time of year?

What was Christmas all about?

I'm not sure how to explain what happened next, only that everything seemed quite natural in its occurrence. The shimmering star that had locked my eyes upon it—a celestial light I knew to exist far, far from my world—suddenly changed perspective, appearing within my sight as if it hovered above me at an arms throw. I blinked a number of times thinking my focus would return to normal and the star would once again hang sensibly in the heavens. Instead, every flitter of my lashes produced a change in the star that revealed with decreasing brightness a male figure centered within the light. He was beautiful beyond description—white, radiant, and smiling down upon me. The thought occurred that I had passed on to the afterlife. Perhaps unawares to my conscious self, I had frozen in the cold and suffered death. Was this radiant being God?

The man's smile broadened as if he found amusement in my thoughts, and I worried he could actually read them. Anxiety made me sink lower, pulling the woolen wrap up over my hair. The blanket warmed me, and so I doubted I was dead.

"Fear not," the man said in the softest voice ever to caress my ears. "Your prayer has been heard." I assumed then he was an angel. To think God would personally come for me was a highly vain notion.

The smiling messenger reached out his hand, and I stared at it, wondering how light appeared to radiate from every inch of his skin. It turned out he stood even closer to me than I had first perceived. I blinked again, disturbed by the way distance seemed an incalculable thing in my eyes.

"Fear not," he repeated. "Take my hand."

Stunned by all the unusualness there was to perceive, I asked, "You heard my prayer?" My forehead tightened at the idea. I didn't recall offering a prayer.

Suddenly, his radiant palm was pressed against my chest. "In here," the angel explained. "*He* knows all your heart's desires."

I wasn't sure whether to attribute it to the glowing touch of an angel or the knowledge that God actually knew me, but a warmth beyond any physical source consumed my chest. All my fears dissipated.

Again a hand was extended to me in offer, and I took hold.

As inept as I had proven myself at perceiving distances, it seemed time and travel also elected

171

to bewilder my senses. For I knew we were in motion, and yet my discernment was of the world revolving around me and my heavenly guide. A whirlwind of chaos encircled us, slowing within a blink to a nighttime sky. I noticed one difference among the stars—a brighter light shone above the others, penetrating the darkness more effectively than any star I had ever witnessed.

"Christmas," the angel breathed, following my gaze upward.

"This is Christmas?" I wondered. "Is this what Christmas is about? A star?"

The angel smiled. "Not entirely." He continued to look up.

"Is it about Heaven?" I asked, broadening my guess.

He flickered a glance at me with his beautiful, bright eyes. "Not entirely."

I watched him as he watched the heavens, the two of us still holding hands, for I was afraid if I attempted to sever our bond I might fall to the ground which we presently hovered above. It wasn't my intent to gawk at him, but withdrawing my eyes proved a difficult thing until something more amazing than a celestial companion lured my focus skyward again.

Singing, rich and harmonic and penetrating, affected me first. Such beautiful carols I had never heard before. As my eyes swept across a choir of angels, I held my breath in awe. They were singing hymns of joyous praise. Carols of a newborn king—the Christ child.

I listened silently, my heart affected so profoundly as to bring tears to my eyes. The whole time my guide squeezed my hand, beaming. It wasn't until the choir began to fade that I noticed a meager audience of sheep and shepherds gathered beneath them, witnessing what I saw.

Then we were all at once standing among the shepherds, mingled in their numbers as if we belonged with them. I could understand their acceptance of me, being wrapped in a woolen blanket that resembled their draped attire, but I knew not why my companion received no incredulous looks. Perhaps because of the messenger angel above?

"Fear not. For behold I bring you good tidings of great joy, which shall be to all people. For unto you is born this day in the city of David, a Savior which is Christ the Lord. And this shall be a sign unto you; ye shall find the babe wrapped in swaddling clothes, lying in a manger."

After a final chorus of praise, the angels went away. I was sad to see them go, to have their inspiring music no longer permeating the atmosphere. Naturally, I sighed at such a stark loss.

My glorious companion sighed likewise. "Ahhh, Christmas."

I nodded. "Is this what Christmas is about? Singing carols and songs of heavenly praise?"

The angel smiled kindly at me. "Not entirely."

"Is it about the message then? Is Christmas about heralding Christ's birth?"

I was given another patient smile. "Not entirely."

We separated from the shepherds, our feet touching the ground now, taking steps on a dirt road. I felt secure enough to let go of my companion's hand. He released my fingers readily. Our walk remained quiet; hushed but for the nocturnal sounds of herding country. I pondered the things that had transpired—the message delivered by heavenly hosts to humble, poor shepherds willing and ready to hear. This was the first Christmas. This was Christ's birthday. What else would Christmas be about if not Him?

I had taken a few steps beyond my angel guide when I realized he was no longer at my side. Turning back, my eyes opened up, aroused from my deep, inner reflecting. We were standing in the shadows of a lowly stable. Stone,

174

wood, and straw were arranged as shelter for docile animals. A small light shone from within, sustained by a single candle. I squinted to make out two silhouettes that appeared joined. Mother and baby.

I couldn't help but ask, whispering, "Is it Him?"

The angel nodded, his smile tempered by reverence.

"This is the first Christmas," I said, making sure my understanding of events was correct.

The angel nodded again, concentrating on the newborn child.

"Christmas is about the baby, Jesus." I declared.

The angel's smile reappeared as a result of my certainty. "Not entirely."

I crumpled my brow, frustrated, but a large shadow distracted my attention, appearing from the back of the stable. A man approached and knelt beside the mother and child. His arm fell gently around the woman, his free hand careful to cup the baby's head. He leaned in to kiss his wife. The picture touched my heart.

"Is Christmas about family?" I asked.

I mouthed the echoed response. "Not entirely."

My eyes flickered from the forms beside a manger to my companion. It was strange that his brilliance didn't light the darkness within the stable. But what *hadn't* proved strange thus far? I was about to question his definition of "entirely" when the scuffing of collected footfall caught my ear. I twisted my neck to find strangers approaching—shepherds in rags and sandals followed by men garbed in finer, richer fabrics.

"The wise men?" I guessed.

My companion nodded.

I watched as the visitors cautiously approached, waiting for permission from the stable's occupants to come close enough to witness the Christ child. I wanted a closer look myself and followed the others across a carpet of strewn straw. I watched the wise men kneel to place gifts at the mother's feet. She appeared truly grateful.

"Is Christmas about gifts?" I asked. It was a holiday tradition spanning the ages, to be sure.

"Not entirely."

The mother, a pretty young woman, held up her baby for all to see. His features were glowing in the candlelight. He was asleep. Adorable. He appeared so tiny and fragile, snuggly wrapped in a single blanket.

"He came to save the world," the angel told me. "To suffer and die for all of us."

I nodded, aware of the truth.

176

"Is that what Christmas is about?" I asked. "Christ's purpose? His suffering and death?"

There was no smile on the angel's face when he turned to me, only gravity in his eyes. "Not entirely."

I sighed. What in the world was Christmas about then? I thought of the few Christmases I had celebrated in my own lifetime—gathered around family, singing carols, exchanging gifts, retelling the story of our Savior's humble birth, rehearsing by heart the angel's tidings of joy to the shepherds. Was this not what Christmas was about?

When the others stepped back, I knelt before the new mother, questioning her with my eyes as to whether or not it would be okay to touch her child. She smiled with understanding and held him out to me, offering the chance to cradle the babe in my arms. I couldn't make myself do it. To hold my savior was a privilege I was unworthy to accept. I yearned, though, to at least touch him. With a trembling reach, I let my hand fall gently against his cheek, so soft and warm. I feared for a moment my touch might be too cold, but the baby stirred and turned his face toward me, his little nose nuzzling in my palm. I exhaled raggedly and chuckled at this. My breathing stopped entirely when his eyes opened up.

He looked right at me.

I couldn't turn away, even when my sight blurred with tears. His tiny fingers moved to wrap around my one, clasping on. Behind him, I caught his mother's smile as she assured me, "He loves you."

I bawled like a baby at her words because I knew they were true. His life, his actions—they proved it to be so.

It took some time to regain my composure before I could speak again. My companion waited patiently for my eyes to dry. He was nodding before I even asked the question.

"Is Christmas about love?"

"It is."

As my angel guide departed to take his place in the heavens, I found myself once again seated on the porch outside my own house. I looked up in time to catch a shooting star. The laughter of friends and family carried to me from inside. Rising to go join them (wondering what the chances were they would believe my miraculous story) I heard the truth proclaimed in the quietest, piercing voice. Words of a loving Father. Words I resolved that very Christmas night to forever abide.

"For I so loved the world that I gave my only begotten Son, that whosoever believeth in Him

should not perish, but have everlasting life. Love one another, even as I have loved you."

December 22nd

The spirit of Christmas exists in melodious carols like those sung by angels on the day of Christ's birth.

December 23rd

Every birthday celebrates a life because every life is important.

December 24th

Maybe Christmas is more than a day to receive. Maybe Christmas, perhaps, is a day to believe.

December 25th

Haiku Christmas Story

New light in the sky
announces a sacred birth.
Shine brightly young star.

Hallelujah song
carries on a gentle wind,
heralding a king.

Shepherds lift their heads,
not to gaze at a new light
but to hear angels.

"Unto you is born
in the city of David
a Savior for all."

Born on straw at night
under low stable rafters,
Baby Jesus cried.

Sheep and goats and cows
gather 'round a manger bed
to awe at a babe.

Wise men come to see
a child of greater wisdom
and honor divine.

Rare and precious gifts,
gold and myrrh and frankincense,
to offer a king.

Mary and Joseph
huddle snugly together.

180

They cradle God's son.

On this wise He came,
the Son of God to the earth.
A humble wonder.

December 26th

Life is the season for loving and caring,
> for laughing and caroling, giving and
> sharing.

Christmas is meant for the same, people say,
> which makes life like Christmastime every
> day.

December 27th

Snowflakes fall from high.
Flurries lift and twirl below.
The world has turned white.

December 28th

Moments always blossom more beautifully in
memories.

December 29ᵗʰ

Time is a power of its own, and it may be the only power by which some miracles come to pass.

December 30ᵗʰ

The only thing you can justifiably claim that life owes you is an equal measure of what you have given out. And even that is debatable.

December 31ˢᵗ

Past and Present I know well; each is a friend and sometimes an enemy to me. But it is the quiet, beckoning Future, an absolute stranger, with whom I have fallen madly in love.

Never judge another knight without first knowing the strength and cunning of the dragons he fights.

~Richelle E. Goodrich

ABOUT THE AUTHOR

Richelle E. Goodrich is native to the Pacific Northwest, born in Utah but raised in Washington State. She lives with her husband and three boys somewhere in a compromise between city and country settings. Richelle graduated from Eastern Washington University with bachelor's degrees in Liberal Studies and Natural Science / Mathematics Education. She loves the arts—drama, sketching, painting, literature—and writes whenever opportunity presents itself. This author describes herself beautifully in the following quote:

"I like bubbles in everything. I respect the power of silence. In cold or warm weather, I favor a mug of hot cocoa. I admire cats— their autonomy, grace, and mystery. I awe at the fiery colors in a sunset. I believe in deity. I hear most often with my eyes, and I will trust a facial expression before any

accompanying comment. I invent rules, words, adventures, and imaginary friends. I pretend something wonderful every day. I will never quit pretending."
                              —Richelle E. Goodrich

OTHER BOOKS BY THIS AUTHOR

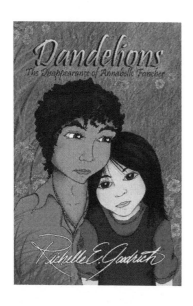

Dandelions: The Disappearance of Annabelle Fancher
by Richelle E. Goodrich

What does a child do when life hurts? She dreams up a hero.
~ A childhood trial of survival.
~ Realism and fantasy beautifully intertwined.

This fictional tale is a suspenseful, human-interest account detailing the harsh reality endured by young Anna. It tenderly acquaints the reader with a lonely young girl and shares her courage facing adversity. Many of the events were taken from the lives of actual people.

Annabelle Fancher lives with her mother and her often-absent, alcoholic father. When he's not on the road, his presence at home instills heightened anxiety in his wife and daughter—fear caused by years of drunken cruelty. Annabelle copes with her circumstances by escaping into storybooks where she dreams characters to life from popular fairytales. There in her dreams she manages to form make-believe moments of happiness.

School is the only place she interacts socially, where a few individuals suspecting her circumstances attempt to reach out to the quiet child; however, it is an imagined friend whom she turns to repeatedly for comfort and kindness. But when his ghostly form appears during waking hours—his voice augmenting the hallucination—it becomes a struggle for Annabelle to keep reality and pretend from blurring boundaries. Her choice, it seems, is to happily succumb to madness or embrace her cruel reality.

Secrets of a Nobel Key Keeper
~ The Story of Dreamland ~
by Richelle E. Goodrich

There are things
that make no sense,
that seem unreal,
that can't be grasped
or understood
or explained,
that maybe don't even exist...
And still, somehow, those wonderful things touch and
change our lives.
Isn't it strange?

Meet a curious, young man whose calling it is to guard
the gates of his homeland. As key keeper of Dreamland,

Gavin comes across many outsiders referred to by his people as dreamers. Through a variety of bizarre and creative antics, Gavin steers these roaming trespassers away from the borders of his magical world—a world where ogres bowl for their dinner, and pirates sail the clouds to plunder diamonds from the night's sky, and bubbleberries make a person burp out loud. It is a place where anything imaginable is commonplace.

All the while, the young key keeper finds himself increasingly intrigued by stories of the outside world. Snooping about, he is captivated by a dreamer who peaks his interest in the ordinary.

This book is supplemental to *Dandelions: The Disappearance of Annabelle Fancher*

Eena, The Dawn and Rescue
by Richelle E. Goodrich

"She was young and beautiful and the last living heir to the throne. Why wouldn't two brothers fight to influence her?"

Sevenah Williams lives a quiet farm life with her parents and best friend, Ian. Life is good and predictable until the unexpected yanks her from the only reality she remembers. Forced from home, her tragic and forgotten past is pieced together revealing that Sevenah is in fact heir to the throne of Harrowbeth; she is the last living of royal blood able to don a peculiar heirloom necklace. Given the new name, Eena, she and Ian set off for a new home, dodging nightmarish enemies in the process. All the while great powers granted by the enchanted necklace slowly emerge and develop.

Eena is assisted by militia sent to retrieve their queen, commanded by the bossy and intimidating Captain Derian. Though Ian and Derian endeavor to protect her, Eena is abducted by a charming, silver-tongued man. She finds herself forced to choose sides in a civil war she hardly understands. Which rival has the power to convince her of his nobleness and gain her ultimate support?

Smile Anyway: Quotes, Verse, & Grumblings for Every Day of the Year
by Richelle E. Goodrich

Smile Anyway is a collection of original quotes, verse, and the occasional grumbling. The book includes a profound thought for every day of the year plus three bonus quotes, including the popular following:

"Anyone who takes the time to be kind is beautiful."

"There are many who don't wish to sleep for fear of nightmares. Sadly, there are many who don't wish to wake for the same fear."

"Gratitude doesn't change the scenery. It merely washes clean the glass you look through so you can clearly see the colors."

"Walk with me awhile, my friend—you in my shoes, I in yours—and then let us talk."

"How often it is we set ourselves in the high seat, judging others, not having read their book but merely having glimpsed the cover."

This book was written to inspire and motivate individuals on a daily basis; it includes a quote for leap year.

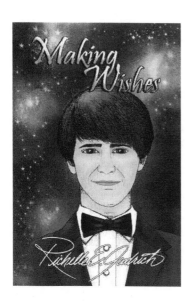

Making Wishes: Quotes, Thoughts, & a Little Poetry for Every Day of the Year
by Richelle E. Goodrich

Making Wishes is a collection of original quotes and poems, including a small number of mini stories. Enjoy a profound thought every day of the year like the popular following:

"Dress yourself in the silks of benevolence because kindness makes you beautiful."

"Don't seek to be happy; let everyone else chase after that rainbow. Seek to be kind, and you'll find the rainbow follows you

"If I must start somewhere, right here and now is the best place imaginable."

"There are times you find yourself standing by the wayside, watching as someone struggles to dig a well with a spoon, and you wish with all your heart you had arms and a shovel."

"Sorrow on another's face often looks like coldness, bitterness, resentment, unfriendliness, apathy, disdain, or disinterest when it is in truth purely sadness."

This book was written to inspire and motivate individuals on a daily basis.

Made in the USA
Middletown, DE
21 April 2017